RETIREMENT PLANNING FOR SINGLE WOMEN

Strategies for Solo Female Retirement Success

Zarek Slade

Copyright © 2024 Zarek Slade

All rights reserved. No part of this publication may be reproduced, distributed, or transmitted in any form or by any means, including photocopying, recording, or other electronic or mechanical methods, without the prior written permission of the publisher, except in the case of brief quotations embodied in critical reviews and certain other noncommercial uses permitted by copyright law.

Table of Contents

Table of Contents... 3
Introduction.. 6
    The Importance of Retirement Planning for Single Women. 7
    Navigating Unique Challenges: Why Solo Retirement is Different... 10
    How This Book Can Guide You Toward a Secure Retirement.. 13
Part 1: Building the Foundation for Financial Security............. 16
    Understanding Your Financial Needs and Goals..................... 16
        Setting Your Retirement Goals: What Does Success Look Like?.. 17
        Calculating Your Target Retirement Income......................21
        Creating a Personalized Retirement Timeline....................24
    Budgeting and Saving for Retirement...................................... 27
        The Power of Budgeting: Managing Today's Finances for Tomorrow's Freedom.. 28
        Savings Strategies for Women: Maximizing Growth on a Single Income.. 30
        Living Below Your Means: Embracing Minimalism and Financial Discipline... 32
    Reducing Debt and Building Wealth... 35
        The Impact of Debt on Retirement Security.......................36
        Proven Strategies for Paying Down Debt Efficiently.......... 39
        Wealth-Building for Single Women: Investments, Real Estate, and Passive Income... 42
Part 2: Growing Your Wealth through Investments................... 45
    Investment Basics for Retirement.. 45
        Introduction to Stocks, Bonds, and Mutual Funds............. 46
        Understanding Risk Tolerance and Investment Goals....... 48
        Building a Balanced Investment Portfolio.......................... 50
    Exploring Investment Options for Single Women....................53
        Real Estate: Is it Right for You?... 54
        Low-Cost Index Funds and ETFs: Simple Strategies for

Growth...57
Understanding Socially Responsible Investing..................59
Navigating Retirement Accounts...61
401(k)s, IRAs, and Roth IRAs: Choosing the Right Account. 63
Maximizing Employer Contributions if Available................ 65
Traditional vs. Roth IRAs: Which is Best for Your Needs?.67

Part 3: Safeguarding Your Future...70
Insurance Essentials for Single Women................................... 70
Health Insurance and Medicare: Planning for Healthcare in Retirement.. 71
Long-Term Care Insurance: Do You Need It?.....................74
Life and Disability Insurance: Planning for the Unexpected... 76
Estate Planning for the Solo Retiree..78
Creating a Will and Power of Attorney................................79
Naming Beneficiaries and Choosing a Guardian................81
Trusts, Executors, and Other Estate Planning Tools......... 83
Managing Social Security and Other Benefits...........................85
Understanding Social Security: Timing and Strategies......86
Maximizing Benefits as a Single Woman...........................88
Supplemental Security Income and Other Government Assistance...90

Part 4: Creating a Lifestyle for a Fulfilling Retirement............... 93
Planning Your Ideal Retirement Lifestyle.................................. 93
Exploring Retirement Hobbies and Interests..................... 94
Building a Support Network: Friends, Community, and Social Engagement...96
Relocating for Retirement: Domestic and International Options..98
Health and Wellness in Retirement.. 101
Staying Active: Physical and Mental Health for Longevity..... 102
Nutrition and Healthy Living on a Retirement Budget...... 104
Accessing Community and Online Resources for Wellness..

      106

  Building Your Retirement Support System............................ 109

      Identifying Trusted Advisors: Financial, Legal, and Medical.. 110

      Building Emotional Resilience for Retirement as a Solo Woman... 112

      Strategies for Avoiding Loneliness and Building New Friendships.. 114

Part 5: Maximizing Your Legacy and Making a Difference........ 117

  Leaving a Legacy as a Single Woman.................................... 117

      Charitable Giving and Philanthropy: How to Get Involved..... 118

      Making a Lasting Impact Through Your Investments and Assets... 120

      Passing Down Knowledge and Values to the Next Generation... 122

  Volunteerism and Giving Back in Retirement......................... 125

      Finding Purpose Through Service.................................... 126

      Becoming a Mentor: Sharing Your Knowledge and Skills 127

      Volunteering Opportunities at Home and Abroad............ 129

Conclusion.. 132

      Embracing the Next Chapter with Confidence and Independence... 133

      Key Takeaways for a Secure and Satisfying Solo Retirement... 135

      Final Words of Encouragement for Single Women Planning Retirement... 136

Introduction

For single women, retirement planning holds a unique set of challenges and considerations that make proactive, thoughtful preparation essential. Unlike traditional retirement planning, which often assumes a dual-income household or a reliance on a partner's pension and benefits, single women approach retirement with the need for complete financial independence. Whether single by choice, circumstance, or as a result of life's unpredictable twists, solo female retirees must navigate the financial landscape differently. Crafting a secure retirement strategy tailored specifically to single women's needs ensures not only financial stability but also the peace of mind that allows for a fulfilling, independent life after leaving the workforce.

This book delves deeply into the core aspects of retirement planning, addressing the unique concerns faced by single women and providing actionable strategies for each stage of preparation. Covering topics from investment choices and estate planning to maximizing Social Security benefits and building a retirement lifestyle that reflects personal passions, this book is designed to empower single women to face retirement with confidence. By understanding the financial realities of retirement and crafting a plan suited to one's individual needs, single women can take control of their futures and create a retirement filled with independence, security, and fulfillment.

The Importance of Retirement Planning for Single Women

Retirement planning for single women is crucial, not only because it provides financial security but also because it ensures a stable and fulfilling retirement lifestyle. Unlike married women who might share retirement costs or benefit from a partner's income and savings, single women face the prospect of supporting themselves entirely. This reality demands a thoughtful, well-structured approach to saving, investing, and budgeting for retirement. Additionally, single women often experience specific financial vulnerabilities such as earning less over their careers due to gender pay gaps or interruptions for caregiving. Such challenges make it imperative to begin retirement planning early, understanding that achieving retirement goals on a single income requires both careful strategizing and informed decision-making.

The first step in understanding the importance of retirement planning for single women is recognizing the financial risks associated with aging independently. Longer life expectancies mean that women generally require larger retirement funds to cover healthcare, housing, and living expenses over an extended period. Women tend to live longer than men, which can result in a more prolonged reliance on retirement savings and a higher likelihood of needing long-term care. Without a retirement plan tailored to these realities, single women may risk outliving their savings or facing financial insecurity during their later years. Financial independence during retirement, therefore, is not just a matter of comfort—it's a necessity to ensure a stable, dignified life free from dependence on limited social services or family support.

Planning for retirement also provides the foundation for maintaining independence and freedom of choice throughout one's later years. With a solid retirement plan, single women can enjoy a lifestyle that reflects their passions, interests, and values, rather than being constrained by financial limitations. Financial preparedness allows for choices, whether it's traveling, pursuing hobbies, relocating, or engaging in community activities. Building this autonomy, however, requires a clear understanding of one's financial situation, realistic budgeting, and disciplined saving habits. It involves regularly assessing financial goals, adjusting for changes in health or income, and making the most of available retirement vehicles like IRAs, 401(k)s, and other investment options. This level of engagement not only helps secure a fulfilling retirement but also creates a sense of empowerment and self-assurance that will be invaluable through retirement.

For single women, planning effectively also requires a proactive approach to health and long-term care costs. Medical expenses often constitute a significant portion of retirement spending, and these expenses can be unpredictable. The burden of healthcare costs can be particularly daunting for single women who lack the support of a spouse to share financial or caregiving responsibilities. Preparing for health-related expenses through health insurance, long-term care insurance, and emergency funds is essential. By understanding potential medical costs and planning accordingly, single women can help protect their savings and maintain their financial health throughout retirement.

An often-overlooked component of retirement planning for single women is estate planning and legacy creation. Even without a spouse or children, many women have loved ones, charitable causes, or specific intentions they wish to honor. A robust retirement plan includes a comprehensive estate plan that clearly outlines how assets will be distributed, who will serve as a healthcare proxy, and other end-of-life decisions. Without this planning, there is a risk that one's legacy will be left to chance, potentially complicating matters for friends, family, or charities left to handle financial and legal issues. Proper planning not only reflects personal values but also preserves the financial and emotional well-being of loved ones.

As the workplace and economy continue to evolve, single women must remain adaptable and informed in their retirement planning strategies. Economic shifts, tax changes, inflation, and shifting financial markets all impact the effectiveness of retirement plans. Financial education and ongoing learning are key to staying prepared for these changes. Staying informed and seeking advice from trusted financial professionals can help single women navigate these challenges, make informed choices, and leverage opportunities that enhance financial growth.

Navigating Unique Challenges: Why Solo Retirement is Different

The experience of retirement is distinctly different for single women compared to those with partners. For solo retirees, financial independence is not merely an ideal but a necessary reality. Single women approach retirement without the benefit of shared household income or joint investments, and this fundamental difference affects every aspect of retirement planning. Living alone and handling all expenses—housing, healthcare, and daily living costs—presents a unique financial challenge that requires careful preparation. Without a second income to fall back on, single women must rely solely on their own savings, investments, and pensions, necessitating meticulous attention to budgeting and long-term financial planning.

Navigating solo retirement also brings emotional and psychological factors into play. In addition to managing finances independently, single retirees often face the challenge of creating a strong support network. While married couples might rely on each other for companionship, healthcare support, and decision-making, single women may need to plan for support in alternative ways. Building a close community of friends, family, or support groups becomes essential, particularly if physical health declines or caregiving needs arise. This aspect of retirement planning is often overlooked, yet it's a critical component for single women aiming to maintain a high quality of life and emotional well-being.

Healthcare costs represent another distinct challenge for single women in retirement. Given that women generally live longer and experience greater healthcare needs as they age, preparing for medical expenses is vital. These costs can be overwhelming without a spouse to share them, leading many single retirees to rely on health savings accounts (HSAs), Medicare, or long-term care insurance. Additionally, single women need to be proactive in researching healthcare providers, understanding Medicare options, and considering potential out-of-pocket expenses that could impact their savings. Taking these steps early helps ensure that healthcare needs are met without diminishing retirement funds intended for living expenses or lifestyle choices.

Estate planning is another area where solo retirement differs significantly. Single women are often responsible for making end-of-life decisions without the input or support of a spouse. This means it's essential to have a well-defined estate plan in place, from selecting an executor to designating healthcare proxies and establishing powers of attorney. Ensuring that one's wishes are respected requires careful documentation and trusted individuals who can help execute plans when necessary. Without a legally binding estate plan, single women risk leaving their assets unprotected or misallocated, which can create additional challenges for any surviving family members or beneficiaries. This type of planning adds peace of mind, knowing that everything is organized and documented.

Financial literacy and ongoing education are especially valuable for single women approaching retirement. Staying informed about investment options, understanding tax implications, and knowing how to maximize Social Security benefits can make a substantial difference in retirement income. Knowledge of these topics allows single women to make informed decisions that contribute to their financial security and independence. Since single women cannot split tax liabilities with a spouse, learning about tax-efficient withdrawal strategies is especially important to minimize the impact of taxes on retirement income.

One of the most rewarding aspects of solo retirement is the freedom to craft a lifestyle that is entirely reflective of personal values, interests, and goals. However, this freedom requires a clear understanding of budget constraints and the discipline to live within them. Planning for travel, hobbies, or personal pursuits requires foresight and realistic financial planning. Establishing a retirement lifestyle based on a carefully crafted budget is empowering and can bring a profound sense of satisfaction and accomplishment. Additionally, for many single women, retirement is an opportunity to volunteer, mentor, or give back to the community in meaningful ways, building a legacy that aligns with their core values.

How This Book Can Guide You Toward a Secure Retirement

This book is a comprehensive guide crafted to address the specific needs and concerns of single women approaching retirement. While traditional retirement resources often overlook the unique challenges faced by solo retirees, this book provides in-depth information and strategies designed to empower single women to plan effectively and confidently. It goes beyond generic financial advice by addressing the distinct realities of retiring independently, from investment choices to healthcare planning, estate preparation, and creating a supportive community network. By focusing on the areas that are most relevant to single women, this book is designed to be a practical and relevant resource, enabling readers to navigate retirement planning with clarity and confidence.

At each step, this book presents clear, actionable guidance that considers the unique financial situation of single women. For example, readers will learn how to maximize retirement savings even if they're starting later in life, manage investments effectively on a single income, and plan for medical expenses and long-term care. With detailed explanations of retirement accounts, Social Security strategies, and investment principles, the book enables readers to make informed decisions that strengthen their financial foundations. Instead of a one-size-fits-all approach, the guidance in this book is tailored to help single women understand how to craft a personalized financial plan that aligns with their specific retirement goals.

A vital part of this guide also addresses the emotional and lifestyle aspects of solo retirement. Retirement is not just about financial stability; it's also about creating a life that is rich in purpose, social connections, and fulfillment. This book provides insights into cultivating a strong social network, staying engaged through meaningful activities, and building emotional resilience. These factors contribute to a healthy, balanced retirement lifestyle and enable single women to enjoy their later years fully. Additionally, practical advice on relocation options, community resources, and health and wellness practices equips readers to design a retirement life that is vibrant, supportive, and aligned with personal aspirations.

Another important component of this book is its focus on estate planning and legacy building. It emphasizes the importance of organizing financial and legal matters to protect one's assets and ensure that personal wishes are respected. For single women, having an estate plan is a way to control the future and provide clarity for loved ones or charitable causes. Detailed chapters on wills, trusts, healthcare proxies, and powers of attorney simplify the estate planning process, making it accessible and actionable.

Throughout, this book encourages a proactive approach. Retirement planning for single women requires foresight, adaptability, and often, creative strategies to maximize financial resources. With a focus on practical solutions, this book demystifies retirement planning and provides readers with the tools and knowledge to take charge of their financial futures. By offering a roadmap for financial security and a fulfilling lifestyle, it allows single women to approach retirement with confidence and optimism. The journey toward a successful solo retirement begins with knowledge, preparation, and a commitment to creating a life that is independent, resilient, and rewarding.

Part 1: Building the Foundation for Financial Security

Understanding Your Financial Needs and Goals

Understanding financial needs and setting clear goals is the foundation for a fulfilling and secure retirement. For single women, this is particularly vital, as the responsibility for maintaining financial independence in retirement rests solely on individual planning. A thorough understanding of financial needs begins with an honest assessment of current income, savings, debts, and monthly expenses, as well as anticipated costs in retirement. This self-assessment provides a realistic view of one's financial landscape and highlights areas requiring adjustments or increased savings. Essential considerations such as housing, healthcare, living expenses, and lifestyle choices form the basis of retirement planning, helping single women create a roadmap for financial stability in their later years. Recognizing these needs early in the process empowers women to make informed choices about savings and investments, giving them greater control over their future.

Establishing financial goals tailored to individual needs and desires is a critical component of retirement planning. Retirement goals should encompass both essential living expenses and personal aspirations, such as travel, hobbies, and charitable endeavors. The financial demands of these goals will vary depending on lifestyle preferences, healthcare needs, and other individual factors. By setting specific, measurable, and attainable goals, single women can gain clarity on the amount needed to achieve financial independence in retirement. Defining these goals not only ensures a comfortable lifestyle but also brings peace of mind, knowing that all aspects of retirement have been thoughtfully considered. Through clear financial understanding and purposeful goal setting, women can confidently pursue a retirement plan that aligns with their values and aspirations.

Setting Your Retirement Goals: What Does Success Look Like?

Defining success in retirement is a deeply personal process that requires careful reflection on lifestyle preferences, values, and ambitions. For single women, achieving a successful retirement may mean different things depending on individual circumstances and desires. Some may envision a retirement filled with travel and exploration, while others may seek a simpler, more tranquil lifestyle closer to family and friends. Whatever the vision, setting specific goals helps create a retirement plan that meets both practical and personal needs. Success in retirement ultimately hinges on the ability to lead a fulfilling and financially secure life, free from financial strain. By understanding what success looks like, women can develop a targeted approach to retirement planning that supports their chosen lifestyle and reflects their unique perspective.

Creating a vision of retirement involves exploring lifestyle desires and understanding how they translate into financial requirements. For instance, a retirement focused on frequent travel will necessitate a different budget than one centered around quiet living in a rural community. A comprehensive plan considers elements such as housing options, preferred activities, social engagement, and personal growth opportunities. Determining these preferences early on provides a framework for retirement savings and investment strategies, ensuring that financial resources align with envisioned retirement goals. This thoughtful approach allows single women to prioritize expenses and focus on building a retirement fund that supports their desired lifestyle.

Health considerations play a substantial role in retirement planning, as they often impact both lifestyle choices and financial needs. Women tend to live longer than men, meaning they may require a larger retirement fund to cover healthcare, housing, and other long-term expenses. Preparing for potential health challenges by incorporating healthcare costs into retirement goals is essential for ensuring financial stability. Planning may include setting aside funds for medical expenses, investing in long-term care insurance, or exploring healthcare savings accounts that provide additional support during retirement. By addressing health-related concerns within retirement goals, single women can feel more secure and better prepared to navigate the uncertainties of aging independently.

Beyond finances, retirement success for single women often includes social engagement and a sense of purpose. Building a fulfilling retirement means planning for connections with others, whether through friendships, community activities, or volunteer work. Retirement can present challenges related to social isolation, especially for those without a partner, so establishing a support network and remaining engaged with community activities can significantly enhance quality of life. Allocating funds for hobbies, travel, or community memberships can provide both social enrichment and emotional well-being. Ensuring that retirement goals include provisions for social activities and personal growth fosters a more balanced and enjoyable lifestyle, creating a retirement experience that is rich in both connection and fulfillment.

Preparing for retirement success also requires flexibility and adaptability. Financial needs and personal goals may shift over time due to unforeseen changes in health, income, or lifestyle preferences. Building flexibility into a retirement plan allows single women to adapt to these changes while maintaining their financial security. Establishing an emergency fund or including buffer funds within retirement savings can provide the financial cushion needed to address unexpected expenses. Furthermore, reassessing and adjusting retirement goals periodically can help single women stay on track, ensuring that their plans remain aligned with their current aspirations and circumstances. A flexible approach enables women to handle life's uncertainties with confidence, preserving their quality of life and financial independence.

Effective retirement planning should also account for legacy considerations and end-of-life planning. Even if there are no direct heirs, many women wish to leave a meaningful legacy, whether through charitable giving, supporting loved ones, or establishing a trust. Including legacy planning within retirement goals not only reflects personal values but also provides clarity on how assets will be managed and distributed. A well-defined estate plan can prevent potential complications and ensure that assets are allocated according to personal wishes. This aspect of retirement planning, often overlooked, can provide a sense of purpose and fulfillment, knowing that one's life and resources continue to make a difference even beyond retirement.

Incorporating these elements into retirement goals allows single women to approach retirement with confidence and clarity. Retirement planning becomes not merely a financial exercise but a holistic strategy for achieving a well-rounded and fulfilling life. By understanding what success looks like and aligning financial resources with personal aspirations, single women can create a retirement experience that is secure, purposeful, and deeply rewarding. Through thoughtful goal setting, they can ensure a retirement that reflects both their values and their vision, enjoying a life of independence and contentment.

Calculating Your Target Retirement Income

Determining target retirement income is essential to ensure financial security and maintain a comfortable lifestyle. Calculating this income involves estimating annual expenses and adjusting for factors such as inflation, healthcare needs, and lifestyle changes. A common guideline is to plan for 70-80% of pre-retirement income, although each individual's requirements will vary based on their chosen retirement lifestyle. By carefully assessing current expenses and projecting future costs, single women can develop a clear understanding of how much income will be needed to support their desired lifestyle in retirement. This calculation provides the foundation for building a retirement savings plan that aligns with personal goals.

To begin estimating retirement income, it is important to analyze current spending patterns and categorize expenses into essential and discretionary costs. Essential expenses include housing, utilities, healthcare, and food, which will remain priorities during retirement. Discretionary spending, on the other hand, covers non-essential items like travel, entertainment, and hobbies. Understanding these categories allows for more accurate budgeting, ensuring that savings cover both basic needs and lifestyle preferences. Single women, in particular, should factor in the cost of living independently, as this can impact expenses related to housing, healthcare, and daily necessities. By prioritizing these expenses, it becomes easier to develop a realistic target income that ensures financial security.

Inflation and rising healthcare costs can significantly impact retirement income needs, especially over a long retirement period. Inflation erodes purchasing power over time, making it crucial to include an inflation-adjusted component in retirement calculations. Additionally, healthcare costs tend to increase with age, and single women may face higher medical expenses due to longer life expectancy and the potential need for long-term care. Incorporating these variables into target income calculations provides a more accurate estimate of the funds required to maintain financial independence. Investment strategies that account for inflation and allocate funds specifically for healthcare can help single women prepare for these future expenses, reducing the risk of financial strain in later years.

Social Security benefits are a primary source of retirement income for many, and understanding how to maximize these benefits is critical for single women. Delaying Social Security claims can increase monthly benefits, providing a higher income over time. Coordinating Social Security benefits with other retirement income sources, such as pensions, IRAs, or

401(k) plans, helps optimize income streams and ensures a stable flow of funds throughout retirement. Calculating target income should include an assessment of when to claim Social Security to achieve the highest possible benefit, as well as a review of other income sources that can supplement these benefits.

Investment income can also play a significant role in meeting retirement income targets. Diversified investment portfolios, which may include stocks, bonds, and real estate, can generate additional income to support retirement goals. Investment strategies should be tailored to individual risk tolerance, age, and time horizon. As retirement approaches, shifting toward a more conservative investment mix may help preserve capital while still generating income. Calculating the potential return from investments, along with Social Security and other income sources, enables single women to estimate their total retirement income. Regularly reviewing and adjusting investment strategies to match changing financial needs ensures that income targets remain achievable.

Creating an income plan that balances essential expenses, healthcare costs, and discretionary spending can help single women achieve financial independence in retirement. By carefully calculating target income and understanding all available income sources, women can build a retirement plan that provides for both basic needs and lifestyle desires. Additionally, an income plan should account for unexpected expenses by incorporating a contingency fund, offering protection against unforeseen financial challenges. Calculating retirement income with a focus on flexibility and sustainability provides single women with a solid foundation for achieving their retirement aspirations.

Creating a Personalized Retirement Timeline

A personalized retirement timeline is a roadmap that guides financial decisions and milestones leading up to retirement. Developing this timeline involves identifying target retirement age, assessing savings goals, and setting benchmarks to track progress. The timeline provides structure and direction, helping single women prioritize financial goals and maintain a clear sense of purpose throughout their working years. An effective timeline incorporates factors such as savings rate, retirement account contributions, and debt reduction, ensuring that each step aligns with retirement aspirations and financial readiness. By creating a customized timeline, single women can take control of their retirement journey and approach each milestone with confidence.

Determining the desired retirement age is a key aspect of developing a retirement timeline. This decision depends on financial readiness, career satisfaction, and lifestyle preferences. Some may wish to retire early to pursue personal interests, while others may aim to work longer for financial security. Establishing a target retirement age provides a timeframe for savings and investment strategies, enabling single women to plan more effectively. This decision also affects Social Security benefits, investment growth potential, and the overall retirement budget. A clear understanding of when retirement is feasible allows women to tailor their timeline according to personal goals and financial resources.

Debt reduction is an important milestone within a retirement timeline, as entering retirement with minimal debt can significantly enhance financial freedom. Reducing debt early in the timeline allows for more focused savings and investment, creating a stronger financial foundation. A personalized timeline includes actionable steps for paying off high-interest debt, such as credit cards or loans, well before retirement. By eliminating financial obligations, single women can allocate more funds toward savings and investments, ultimately boosting retirement income. Reaching debt-free status is a critical benchmark in any retirement timeline, providing greater peace of mind and financial flexibility.

Retirement account contributions, including 401(k)s, IRAs, and other tax-advantaged accounts, play a central role in building retirement savings. Regular contributions, employer matching, and catch-up contributions for those over age 50 can accelerate savings growth. A personalized timeline includes goals for maximizing contributions, allowing single women to take full advantage of these accounts. Incorporating specific milestones, such as reaching annual contribution limits, helps track progress and ensures consistent savings efforts. As retirement approaches, gradually shifting investments to more conservative options can help preserve capital and reduce risk, providing stability and security within the timeline.

Periodic reviews of retirement progress are essential for maintaining momentum and adjusting strategies as needed. Life circumstances, economic changes, and financial goals can shift over time, making flexibility a valuable asset within a retirement timeline. Conducting annual or bi-annual assessments helps single women stay on course, identifying areas for improvement and celebrating milestones achieved. Reviewing and recalibrating savings goals, investment strategies, and retirement income projections ensures that the timeline remains relevant and effective. This continuous improvement approach strengthens financial resilience, allowing women to approach retirement with confidence and a clear sense of accomplishment.

Creating a personalized retirement timeline empowers single women to actively shape their financial future, establishing a path toward a secure and fulfilling retirement. By mapping out each milestone and setting achievable goals, women can feel prepared and optimistic as they move toward retirement. A well-structured timeline not only fosters financial independence but also reinforces a sense of control and direction, ensuring that retirement planning remains a proactive and rewarding journey. Through a clear timeline and consistent progress, single women can confidently embrace retirement, knowing they have laid the groundwork for a successful and satisfying life ahead.

Budgeting and Saving for Retirement

Budgeting and saving for retirement are especially crucial for single women, who often bear the full responsibility of securing their financial futures. Developing a solid budget forms the foundation of this effort, providing a structured approach to manage expenses, prioritize savings, and set clear financial goals. A well-crafted budget not only helps maintain discipline in day-to-day spending but also supports a long-term vision of retirement security. By allocating a portion of income to retirement accounts and high-yield savings early on, single women can build a financial buffer that grows over time, helping offset challenges such as inflation and unexpected costs.

Beyond simply monitoring expenses, budgeting enables single women to proactively plan for emergencies, such as medical issues or housing repairs, which can otherwise disrupt financial stability. Incorporating an emergency fund into the budget creates a safeguard, offering peace of mind and preserving retirement savings even in the face of unforeseen events. Moreover, understanding personal spending patterns through regular tracking makes it easier to identify opportunities to redirect funds from non-essential expenses to retirement savings. Through consistent budgeting and a commitment to saving, single women can build a resilient financial plan that prepares them for a comfortable and independent retirement.

The Power of Budgeting: Managing Today's Finances for Tomorrow's Freedom

A strong budget promotes freedom and independence in retirement by fostering financial stability in the present. For single women, managing today's finances carefully sets the stage for a self-sufficient and stress-free future. One of the most compelling advantages of budgeting is its ability to build confidence in handling personal finances, ensuring that all expenditures align with the ultimate retirement goal. A disciplined approach to budgeting means consciously evaluating purchases and considering long-term impact rather than succumbing to immediate desires. Over time, this conscious approach cultivates a mindset of frugality and strategic thinking, essential qualities for financial success.

Implementing a budget encourages better control over monthly cash flow and empowers women to track every expense, from household bills to discretionary spending. Detailed tracking makes it easier to differentiate between essential and non-essential expenses, creating an awareness of spending patterns that may otherwise go unnoticed. Single women who adopt this habit find it easier to prioritize necessary expenditures and avoid impulsive spending. This focus on essentials allows for more efficient use of available resources, ultimately freeing up funds for retirement savings and other financial goals. With each expense scrutinized for its value and necessity, budgeting becomes a deliberate practice that nurtures fiscal responsibility and forward-thinking.

Furthermore, budgeting enables women to set realistic, achievable financial goals. Breaking down retirement savings into manageable monthly or yearly targets can make the process feel less daunting, providing clear objectives and a sense of direction. Through disciplined adherence to a budget, women can visualize their progress and make incremental advancements toward retirement security. For example, a single woman with a goal of saving $500,000 for retirement can calculate monthly contributions needed to reach that target within a specific timeline. This approach provides motivation, as each step forward reinforces the progress being made, bringing retirement goals closer to reality. Budgeting provides a roadmap, helping single women navigate financial challenges and remain steadfast on the journey toward long-term freedom.

Budgeting also helps balance retirement savings with other financial priorities, such as debt repayment or short-term savings goals. Single women may need to balance paying down student loans, mortgages, or credit card debt while saving for retirement, making efficient resource allocation essential. A well-planned budget provides flexibility to address these priorities without compromising retirement contributions. By creating a strategy that allocates a portion of income toward debt repayment while maintaining a steady retirement savings rate, single women can achieve a balance that supports both immediate and future financial stability.

Savings Strategies for Women: Maximizing Growth on a Single Income

Building retirement savings on a single income presents unique challenges, but with strategic planning and disciplined savings practices, single women can still achieve substantial financial growth. The key to successful saving lies in finding high-yield opportunities that maximize income while minimizing risk. Contributions to tax-advantaged retirement accounts, such as a 401(k) or IRA, are a cornerstone of any savings strategy. These accounts offer benefits such as tax deductions, tax-deferred growth, or tax-free withdrawals, depending on the type of account, helping to optimize retirement savings. Consistently contributing to these accounts allows for exponential growth over time, taking advantage of compound interest to build a robust nest egg.

In addition to traditional retirement accounts, diversified investments can amplify savings potential. Single women may consider a portfolio that balances stocks, bonds, and mutual funds, adapting as they approach retirement age. Younger women might opt for a more aggressive portfolio with a higher stock allocation, while those nearing retirement might shift to bonds or other safer assets to protect against market volatility. Investing in index funds or exchange-traded funds (ETFs) can provide broad market exposure and lower fees, which can be beneficial when managing investments independently. Through diversified, low-cost investment options, single women can pursue growth with a well-rounded strategy that aligns with personal risk tolerance and long-term goals.

Automated savings plans can be a practical solution for ensuring consistency in retirement contributions. Automated contributions, whether through an employer-sponsored plan or a personal retirement account, remove the temptation to skip contributions and make saving for retirement a priority. Setting up an automatic monthly transfer to a high-yield savings account, Roth IRA, or brokerage account ensures that savings continue to grow regardless of fluctuations in income or spending habits. This approach allows single women to build retirement funds consistently, minimizing the impact of lifestyle changes or unexpected financial demands.

Managing and reducing unnecessary expenses can also significantly contribute to retirement savings on a single income. Small but consistent changes, such as limiting dining out, cutting cable subscriptions, or reducing transportation costs, can lead to substantial savings over time. These saved amounts, however modest, can be redirected into retirement accounts or invested in growth opportunities, ultimately enhancing retirement preparedness. For single women who may not have the financial support of a partner, frugality and cost-cutting are essential elements of a successful retirement savings strategy.

Saving strategies should also include building an emergency fund to provide a financial safety net. An emergency fund protects against unforeseen expenses, such as medical bills or home repairs, without requiring retirement withdrawals or increased debt. Single women, who may not have a dual-income household to rely on, benefit greatly from the security an emergency fund offers. By setting aside three to six months' worth of living expenses in a separate account, women can manage life's unexpected events with confidence, knowing their retirement savings remain untouched.

Living Below Your Means: Embracing Minimalism and Financial Discipline

Living below one's means is a powerful approach to building a stable financial future and achieving retirement success. Adopting a minimalist lifestyle and practicing financial discipline can accelerate retirement savings, allowing single women to reach financial independence sooner. Living below one's means entails making conscious choices about spending, prioritizing needs over wants, and recognizing the value of delayed gratification. For single women, embracing this philosophy not only enhances financial stability but also fosters a sense of control and self-reliance, as each financial decision contributes to long-term security.

Minimalism, in a financial sense, does not necessarily mean sacrificing enjoyment or quality of life. Rather, it involves making thoughtful choices that align with long-term goals and focusing on experiences or possessions that genuinely add value. This approach allows for a reduction in unnecessary expenses and promotes a mindful lifestyle. For example, choosing to buy a smaller home or renting instead of purchasing allows for lower housing expenses, freeing up funds for retirement savings. Opting for second-hand items, limiting luxury purchases, and focusing on value-driven spending can make a significant impact over time, allowing for consistent contributions to retirement accounts.

Living below one's means also extends to debt management, as minimizing debt allows for greater financial freedom. High-interest debt, such as credit cards, can quickly erode savings and limit retirement contributions. Single women aiming for financial independence can prioritize paying off debt as part of their commitment to minimalism and disciplined living. The sooner high-interest debt is eliminated, the more income can be allocated toward saving and investing. By embracing a debt-free lifestyle, women gain peace of mind and ensure that more of their hard-earned money contributes to a secure retirement.

Financial discipline is crucial when living on a single income, as it requires careful planning and consistent savings habits. Practicing restraint in discretionary spending and focusing on financial priorities builds resilience and helps navigate challenges that may arise. Financial discipline also involves periodic reviews of personal finances to ensure alignment with retirement goals, making adjustments as necessary to stay on track. This proactive approach cultivates a mindset of responsibility and foresight, which is invaluable for single women working toward a financially secure retirement.

Embracing minimalism and financial discipline also fosters a sense of purpose, as each financial decision contributes directly to the goal of independence in retirement. When spending aligns with values and long-term aspirations, retirement savings become a source of motivation rather than a chore. Viewing minimalism as a lifestyle choice rather than a restriction transforms budgeting and saving into meaningful, purposeful actions. For single women, each saved dollar brings them one step closer to achieving a fulfilling and self-sufficient retirement, underscoring the connection between present sacrifices and future freedom.

Living below one's means not only supports financial growth but also promotes adaptability, a quality that is especially beneficial in retirement. Retiring on a budget or living with limited resources becomes more manageable for those who have already embraced minimalism. This approach builds resilience and flexibility, making it easier to adjust to potential shifts in income or lifestyle in retirement. For instance, those accustomed to a frugal lifestyle may find it easier to stretch retirement savings over an extended period, ensuring a comfortable and enjoyable retirement without the need for substantial income.

By living below their means, single women can empower themselves to create a retirement plan that is not dependent on external support or income. Embracing a minimalist approach, combined with consistent budgeting and disciplined saving, creates a foundation for a rewarding retirement built on independence, security, and peace of mind.

Reducing Debt and Building Wealth

Reducing debt and building wealth are essential components of financial security, especially for single women planning for a secure retirement. Debt reduction creates a stable foundation, allowing savings and investments to grow without the burden of high-interest obligations. Eliminating debt, particularly high-interest debt, increases disposable income, freeing up resources that can then be allocated to savings and investments. This financial freedom enables single women to focus on their wealth-building efforts, whether through investment portfolios, property ownership, or passive income opportunities. In this way, minimizing debt serves as a precursor to financial growth, empowering single women to move forward with a sense of independence and control over their financial future.

Building wealth goes beyond simply earning and saving; it involves making strategic financial decisions that promote long-term stability and growth. Wealth-building provides the potential for financial freedom, even in retirement, allowing single women to maintain their lifestyle without the need for outside support. By focusing on reducing debt and increasing assets through smart investments, retirement accounts, and income-generating opportunities, single women can create a strong, self-sustaining financial foundation. Combining debt elimination with wealth-building not only reinforces financial security but also allows single women to enter retirement with confidence, knowing they have laid the groundwork for a fulfilling and financially sound future.

The Impact of Debt on Retirement Security

Debt has a significant impact on retirement security, as it can hinder both the ability to save and the freedom to allocate resources toward future needs. High-interest debt, such as credit card balances or personal loans, drains income that could otherwise be directed toward retirement savings, effectively reducing the potential for financial growth over time. This scenario can be particularly challenging for single women, as managing debt independently requires consistent financial discipline and careful planning. Entering retirement with substantial debt diminishes the stability that is crucial for financial security, as monthly debt payments may consume a significant portion of income, leaving less available for essential expenses and quality-of-life enhancements. To achieve a stable retirement, reducing or eliminating debt well before retirement age is essential, as it allows for a greater allocation of resources toward savings and investments, thereby enhancing retirement security.

The psychological impact of debt also affects retirement planning, as the burden of financial obligations can create stress and limit confidence in financial decision-making. When single women are solely responsible for debt repayment, the pressures can intensify, potentially leading to decisions that focus on short-term relief rather than long-term growth. This cycle can make it difficult to set aside adequate savings for retirement, as immediate debt payments take precedence over future needs. Additionally, high debt levels can lower one's credit score, affecting access to low-interest financing options for larger investments, such as real estate. These factors collectively create barriers to wealth-building, limiting the opportunities for financial growth that are essential to retirement security. The path to a stable retirement is greatly enhanced when debt levels are minimal, as low or eliminated debt translates into financial freedom and a greater capacity to focus on investments that yield long-term benefits.

Debt can also delay retirement by increasing the need for additional income to cover expenses. Single women who enter retirement with unresolved debt may find it necessary to continue working longer or take on part-time employment to supplement their income. This dependency on employment creates uncertainty, as future health or job market changes may disrupt income sources. With debt obligations, the option of an early retirement becomes increasingly difficult to achieve, as ongoing payments limit financial flexibility and add pressure to extend one's working years. Reducing debt as part of a retirement plan not only protects against such disruptions but also enables single women to transition into retirement with a sense of financial freedom and self-reliance.

Furthermore, debt payments can erode the purchasing power of retirement savings, reducing the funds available for essentials such as housing, healthcare, and recreational activities. Inflation, combined with ongoing debt payments, can create financial strain during retirement, as a fixed or limited income may not keep pace with rising costs. Reducing or eliminating debt ensures that retirement savings retain their intended purchasing power, allowing single women to maintain their quality of life without the need to allocate funds toward past obligations. This focus on debt reduction before retirement safeguards both financial and personal well-being, enhancing the likelihood of a fulfilling and stable retirement.

Proven Strategies for Paying Down Debt Efficiently

Effective debt repayment strategies are crucial for achieving financial freedom and securing a comfortable retirement. One of the most widely recommended approaches is the "debt avalanche" method, which prioritizes paying off high-interest debt first. This method focuses on debts with the highest interest rates, allowing single women to reduce the overall cost of debt over time. By concentrating on these high-cost debts, the avalanche method minimizes the amount of interest paid, freeing up additional resources for savings and investments. Once the highest-interest debt is eliminated, attention can shift to debts with lower interest rates, creating a cascading effect that accelerates the overall debt repayment process. This approach is especially beneficial for single women aiming to optimize their financial resources and enter retirement debt-free.

The "debt snowball" method is another popular approach that can be effective, especially for those who benefit from motivation gained by small victories. This method involves paying off the smallest debt balances first, regardless of interest rates, to build momentum and a sense of accomplishment. Each paid-off debt provides positive reinforcement, encouraging further progress toward eliminating remaining balances. By tackling small debts first, single women can quickly reduce the number of financial obligations, simplifying their financial situation and enabling a greater focus on larger debts. Although this method may incur higher interest costs than the avalanche approach, it can offer psychological benefits and a structured path toward financial independence, particularly for those seeking motivation through immediate results.

Consolidation is another efficient strategy for managing multiple debts, as it combines several debts into a single, lower-interest loan. By consolidating credit card balances or personal loans, single women can streamline debt repayment and often reduce their monthly payments, freeing up additional funds for savings. This strategy works best when the consolidation loan carries a lower interest rate than the original debts, as it lowers the overall cost of debt over time. Debt consolidation is especially helpful for those managing multiple high-interest obligations, as it simplifies financial management and supports consistent progress toward debt elimination. When executed with a clear repayment plan, debt consolidation can be an effective tool for reducing financial stress and accelerating the journey to a debt-free future.

Budget adjustments are also essential for efficient debt repayment, as they create a structured approach to managing income and expenses. By identifying discretionary expenses that can be reduced or eliminated, single women can allocate additional funds toward debt repayment each month. Simple lifestyle changes, such as cooking meals at home or limiting entertainment expenses, can collectively contribute to significant debt reduction. Building a realistic budget that includes specific debt repayment goals encourages discipline and consistency, ensuring that monthly payments remain on track and progress is made. For single women focused on achieving financial independence, budgeting becomes a valuable tool in accelerating debt reduction and strengthening financial stability.

Increasing income through side hustles, freelance work, or part-time employment can also expedite debt repayment. Supplementing one's primary income with additional earnings creates more financial resources that can be directed toward debt reduction. This approach allows single women to address their debt more aggressively, shortening the repayment timeline and reducing the impact of interest costs. For those with specialized skills, freelance opportunities or consulting work can provide a flexible source of income, enhancing both financial security and the ability to achieve a debt-free status. By proactively seeking ways to increase income, single women can accelerate their financial goals and build a stronger foundation for retirement.

Wealth-Building for Single Women: Investments, Real Estate, and Passive Income

Wealth-building offers single women the opportunity to secure a stable financial future, empowering them to approach retirement with confidence and independence. Investments play a fundamental role in building wealth, as they provide the potential for growth beyond what traditional savings accounts can offer. Stocks, bonds, and mutual funds are accessible investment options that allow single women to diversify their portfolios and reduce risk while pursuing financial growth. Stocks offer potential for substantial returns, though they carry higher risk, while bonds provide stable income and lower volatility. A balanced portfolio that includes both asset classes allows for gradual, sustainable wealth accumulation, supporting long-term retirement goals. For single women planning for the future, consistent investment contributions form the cornerstone of a robust retirement plan, creating a pathway to financial security.

Real estate investment is another powerful wealth-building strategy, as it provides both passive income and long-term asset appreciation. Rental properties, for example, generate a steady income stream that can supplement retirement savings and enhance financial stability. Property ownership also offers tax benefits and the potential for property value growth, creating an asset that can be sold, rented, or passed down. While real estate investment requires an initial capital outlay, it offers the opportunity for financial returns that contribute to overall wealth-building. For single women looking to diversify income sources, real estate offers both stability and growth potential, enabling them to build wealth that supports a comfortable and fulfilling retirement.

Passive income streams, such as dividends, royalties, or income from digital products, offer additional opportunities to build wealth and increase retirement security. Dividend-paying stocks provide regular income distributions that can be reinvested or used to supplement monthly expenses, enhancing both savings and income potential. For single women with creative or professional skills, royalties from books, digital products, or online courses offer a source of income that requires minimal ongoing effort once established. Passive income not only contributes to wealth accumulation but also enhances financial resilience, creating a buffer against market fluctuations and economic uncertainties. By establishing multiple income streams, single women can create a diversified income portfolio that supports long-term stability and mitigates the risk of relying on a single source of income.

Investing in retirement accounts, such as a 401(k) or an IRA, provides tax advantages that enhance wealth-building efforts. Contributions to a traditional 401(k) or IRA are tax-deferred, allowing investments to grow over time without immediate tax implications, while Roth accounts offer tax-free growth and withdrawals. By maximizing contributions to these accounts, single women can take advantage of compound interest and reduce their taxable income, increasing the value of their retirement savings. Consistent contributions, employer matches, and strategic asset allocation within these accounts support the goal of building a retirement fund that provides financial freedom and independence.

With a strategic focus on reducing debt and building wealth through diversified investments, real estate, and passive income, single women can create a stable financial future that enables them to approach retirement with confidence. By eliminating high-interest debt, strategically investing in assets that align with their goals, and developing multiple income streams, single women can build wealth independently, ensuring that retirement becomes a time of security, stability, and fulfillment.

Part 2: Growing Your Wealth through Investments

Investment Basics for Retirement

Investing is a powerful tool for building a secure retirement, as it provides the potential for financial growth beyond what traditional savings alone can achieve. For single women, investing with a focus on retirement goals enables greater financial independence and allows for a more comfortable lifestyle in later years. A basic understanding of investment principles helps to form a foundation for making informed decisions that align with individual goals, risk tolerance, and retirement timelines. At its core, investing involves placing money in assets that have the potential to increase in value or generate income over time, creating a solid financial base that supports long-term stability.

The foundation of retirement investing lies in understanding the different types of assets available, how they perform, and how they fit into a well-rounded portfolio. Each investment type offers unique benefits, challenges, and risks. Stocks, bonds, and mutual funds represent some of the primary options within the investment landscape, each serving a specific role in contributing to a diversified retirement portfolio. While stocks offer the potential for higher returns, they also come with greater volatility. Bonds provide stability and income but may yield lower returns, especially over the short term. Mutual funds, combining various assets within a single portfolio, offer a middle ground that balances growth potential with diversification. A clear understanding of these basic investment types and how they can be blended helps single women build a retirement portfolio that reflects both their financial goals and their comfort with risk.

Introduction to Stocks, Bonds, and Mutual Funds

Stocks represent ownership in a company, making them a foundational investment vehicle for those seeking long-term growth. When purchasing a stock, investors buy a piece of a company, meaning they share in its profits and losses. This ownership allows investors to benefit when the company performs well, often resulting in an increase in stock value. However, stocks can be volatile, with their prices influenced by factors such as economic conditions, market trends, and corporate performance. Over time, stocks have historically provided higher returns than other types of investments, making them a popular choice for individuals with a long retirement timeline. For single women planning for retirement, stocks offer the potential for significant growth, though it is essential to recognize the possibility of fluctuations along the way.

Bonds, on the other hand, are generally considered a safer investment, as they are debt instruments issued by governments, corporations, or municipalities. When purchasing a bond, an investor is essentially lending money to the issuer in exchange for periodic interest payments and the return of the principal at the bond's maturity. Bonds are often used as a stabilizing element within a portfolio, as they provide consistent income and are less volatile than stocks. Though bonds may offer lower returns, their predictable nature can be beneficial, especially for those nearing retirement who wish to protect their capital. Additionally, there are various types of bonds, such as government bonds, corporate bonds, and municipal bonds, each carrying unique benefits and risks. Understanding the role of bonds within a retirement strategy is important for single women seeking a balance between income and preservation of capital.

Mutual funds serve as an efficient way to gain exposure to a diversified portfolio of stocks, bonds, or a combination of both. These funds pool money from multiple investors to purchase a wide range of assets, offering the benefits of professional management and broad diversification. By investing in a mutual fund, single women can reduce the impact of individual stock or bond performance on their portfolio, as the fund holds many assets that balance each other out. Mutual funds are available in various forms, including equity funds (focused on stocks), fixed-income funds (focused on bonds), and balanced funds (combining stocks and bonds). The diversity within mutual funds makes them an appealing choice for those seeking to build a balanced retirement portfolio without needing to manage individual stocks or bonds. For those new to investing, mutual funds provide a low-maintenance approach that offers both growth and stability.

Beyond these primary types of investments, exchange-traded funds (ETFs) also play a significant role in retirement portfolios. ETFs are similar to mutual funds in that they hold a diversified portfolio of assets, but they trade on stock exchanges like individual stocks. ETFs offer flexibility, as they can be bought and sold throughout the trading day, and often have lower fees than mutual funds. Their structure makes them an efficient way to access different market sectors, industries, or asset classes within a single investment. For single women focused on low-cost, flexible investment options, ETFs can provide an additional layer of diversification and convenience. Building a retirement portfolio that incorporates stocks, bonds, mutual funds, and ETFs offers an array of growth and income options, helping to secure a more stable financial future.

Understanding Risk Tolerance and Investment Goals

Understanding risk tolerance is an essential aspect of investing, as it determines the types of assets that will best align with an individual's comfort level and financial objectives. Risk tolerance varies from person to person and can be influenced by factors such as age, income level, financial goals, and personal preferences. Single women planning for retirement benefit from assessing their risk tolerance, as it provides a guide for selecting appropriate investments that match both their financial situation and emotional comfort. Those with a high tolerance for risk may be comfortable with a portfolio heavy in stocks, which offers the potential for high returns but also carries greater volatility. In contrast, those with a low tolerance for risk may prefer bonds or conservative mutual funds, which provide stability but may yield lower returns over time.

Investment goals also play a central role in shaping a retirement strategy, as they define the purpose and timeline for each financial decision. For single women focused on retirement, establishing clear goals helps in determining the ideal balance of growth and security within a portfolio. Some may aim for a specific retirement age, while others prioritize achieving a certain level of savings to support their desired lifestyle. Having a well-defined goal encourages disciplined saving and investment, ensuring that financial decisions align with long-term objectives. Single women who begin investing early in their careers may prioritize aggressive growth, while those closer to retirement age might focus on preserving wealth and generating income. By clarifying both risk tolerance and investment goals, it becomes easier to build a portfolio that meets both immediate and future needs.

As retirement nears, reassessing risk tolerance and goals becomes essential to ensure that the portfolio continues to align with evolving financial requirements.

While a younger investor may prioritize growth through a high allocation to stocks, an individual approaching retirement may shift focus to more stable assets such as bonds and dividend-paying stocks. This transition reflects the need to protect accumulated wealth while ensuring a steady income during retirement. Understanding one's changing risk tolerance allows single women to make timely adjustments to their portfolio, optimizing returns while safeguarding against unnecessary risk. Balancing risk tolerance and investment goals creates a stable foundation for retirement planning, supporting both financial growth and peace of mind.

Building a Balanced Investment Portfolio

Building a balanced investment portfolio is a strategic approach to retirement planning, as it offers both growth potential and protection against market fluctuations. A balanced portfolio typically includes a mix of asset classes, such as stocks, bonds, and cash, to achieve diversification. By spreading investments across different types of assets, single women can reduce the impact of any single asset's poor performance on the overall portfolio. For example, when the stock market is volatile, bonds may provide stability and income, cushioning the portfolio against sudden losses. This balance between growth and income-generating assets creates a more resilient portfolio that can weather market shifts and support long-term financial goals.

In addition to selecting a diverse range of asset classes, a balanced portfolio also involves strategic asset allocation, or the specific percentage assigned to each asset type. Asset allocation reflects individual risk tolerance, investment goals, and retirement timelines. For example, a younger investor with a high-risk tolerance might allocate a larger portion of the portfolio to stocks, maximizing growth potential over time. Conversely, someone nearing retirement may prioritize a higher allocation to bonds and dividend-paying stocks to generate income and reduce exposure to volatility. Adjusting asset allocation as retirement approaches ensures that the portfolio remains aligned with evolving financial priorities and risk tolerance, supporting both security and growth throughout different life stages.

Rebalancing the portfolio periodically is essential to maintaining the desired asset allocation. Market fluctuations can shift the balance of assets within the portfolio, leading to an unintended increase or decrease in exposure to specific types of investments. For example, if stocks perform exceptionally well, they may come to represent a larger percentage of the portfolio, increasing its risk level. Rebalancing involves selling some assets that have grown beyond their target allocation and reallocating funds to underrepresented assets. This practice keeps the portfolio aligned with the original investment strategy, ensuring that it continues to reflect both financial goals and risk tolerance. Regular rebalancing supports the stability of the portfolio and prevents an overconcentration in any single asset type, enhancing long-term growth and security.

An important consideration in building a balanced portfolio is to include international investments, which add a layer of geographic diversification. Investing in international stocks and bonds provides exposure to markets outside of one's home country, reducing dependency on any single economy. For single women planning for retirement, international investments offer growth opportunities in emerging and developed markets, potentially boosting overall returns while spreading risk. Although international investments can introduce currency fluctuations and geopolitical risks, they also offer access to diverse sectors and industries, enhancing the portfolio's resilience. A balanced portfolio that incorporates both domestic and international assets provides additional growth potential, creating a well-rounded investment strategy for long-term security.

Dividend-paying stocks and income-generating assets such as real estate investment trusts (REITs) also play a valuable role in a balanced portfolio. Dividend stocks provide regular income distributions, offering both growth and cash flow that can be reinvested or used to cover expenses in retirement. REITs, which focus on income from real estate properties, offer a steady income stream and diversification away from traditional stocks and bonds. Including these types of assets within a retirement portfolio supports the goal of generating consistent income, particularly during retirement when stability becomes a priority. For single women seeking financial independence in retirement, income-generating investments enhance the portfolio's overall stability, ensuring a steady cash flow to support their lifestyle.

By thoughtfully constructing a balanced portfolio that incorporates diverse asset classes, single women can create a stable foundation for a secure retirement. Balancing growth-oriented stocks with income-focused bonds and dividend investments provides both resilience and income, enabling individuals to navigate market shifts with confidence. A balanced approach to retirement investing promotes long-term financial security, empowering single women to enjoy independence and freedom throughout their retirement years.

Exploring Investment Options for Single Women

For single women, financial independence and long-term security often center on making smart investment decisions tailored to individual goals, lifestyle preferences, and values. While traditional methods of saving, such as depositing into a savings account, remain vital, they generally fall short of providing the growth needed for a comfortable retirement. Investing, by contrast, offers the potential for wealth accumulation, allowing savings to work harder and grow over time. With so many investment options available, selecting the right ones requires understanding both personal financial needs and the unique advantages each investment provides. Real estate, low-cost index funds, exchange-traded funds (ETFs), and socially responsible investing (SRI) are among the most popular options that align well with the needs of single women seeking long-term growth, stability, and meaningful financial returns.

These investment options are diverse, catering to varying risk tolerances and personal values. Real estate appeals to those seeking tangible assets and potential passive income, while low-cost index funds and ETFs offer a straightforward path to growth with relatively low fees. Socially responsible investing is particularly appealing for those interested in aligning financial growth with social values, giving investors a way to support environmental, social, and governance (ESG) goals through their investment choices. Each approach has distinct features, offering a mix of risk, reward, and personal alignment with values, which makes selecting a combination of these options ideal for achieving a diversified and resilient portfolio. By exploring and understanding these choices, single women can create a financial strategy that aligns with both their economic goals and their principles.

Real Estate: Is it Right for You?

Real estate can be a compelling investment for single women looking to diversify their portfolios and generate additional income streams. Property investments can offer both growth in value over time and regular income if rented out. Real estate holds an intrinsic value, as it provides physical assets that are generally less susceptible to market volatility than stocks. For investors with long-term perspectives, real estate can appreciate significantly, offering substantial returns, especially in regions where property values are steadily rising. Owning rental properties, for instance, enables investors to benefit from regular rental income while building equity as the property's value appreciates. Additionally, rental income provides a source of cash flow that can be particularly beneficial during retirement when stable income streams are a priority. However, managing real estate requires both time and knowledge, as property management can involve responsibilities like maintenance, tenant management, and legal compliance.

While real estate investments offer potential for strong returns, they also come with certain challenges and risks. Purchasing property often involves a significant upfront financial commitment, requiring a down payment, closing costs, and other expenses such as maintenance and property taxes. Real estate is not a liquid asset, meaning it cannot be quickly sold or converted to cash without potential losses, particularly in a down market. This illiquidity can be challenging for those who may need immediate access to funds. Financing a property can also involve navigating mortgage processes, interest rates, and varying real estate market conditions, which can impact the property's long-term value. Furthermore, managing rental properties is not without risk. Tenants can default on rent, unexpected repairs can arise, and property values can fluctuate based on market trends. Despite these considerations, for those comfortable with a hands-on investment, real estate can be a valuable component of a diversified portfolio, especially if properties are chosen carefully in growth areas and managed effectively.

There are also alternative ways to invest in real estate without the direct management responsibilities of physical property ownership. Real estate investment trusts (REITs) allow investors to buy shares in a diversified portfolio of real estate assets, providing exposure to commercial, residential, and industrial properties. REITs are publicly traded, making them more liquid than physical property, as shares can be bought and sold easily on the stock market. REITs offer a way to access real estate's income-generating potential without the need to manage property directly. Many REITs also pay out regular dividends, which can contribute to a steady income stream. For single women who value real estate as an asset class but prefer not to engage in property management, REITs provide a convenient, low-maintenance option that still offers exposure to real estate's growth and income potential.

Low-Cost Index Funds and ETFs: Simple Strategies for Growth

Index funds and ETFs are appealing investment options for single women due to their low fees, ease of management, and broad market exposure. These investment vehicles track specific indexes, such as the S&P 500, and allow investors to hold a diversified portfolio that mirrors the performance of the overall market or a specific sector. Index funds are passively managed, meaning they aim to match the returns of an index rather than outperform it, which helps to keep costs low. This low-cost structure makes them an excellent choice for long-term growth, as lower fees translate into more money compounding over time. For single women looking to build wealth in a straightforward and cost-effective manner, index funds provide an ideal blend of growth potential and simplicity.

ETFs function similarly to index funds in that they track a specific index and offer a diversified portfolio within a single investment. However, ETFs trade on the stock exchange like individual stocks, which provides flexibility in buying and selling shares throughout the trading day. This flexibility makes ETFs particularly attractive for investors who want the option to react to market movements. Like index funds, ETFs have low management fees, which helps to maximize returns over the long term. Because they are diversified, both index funds and ETFs reduce the risk associated with individual stocks, providing a stable foundation for a retirement portfolio. Additionally, many ETFs offer exposure to specific sectors or themes, such as technology, healthcare, or environmental sustainability, allowing investors to target areas they believe have strong growth potential or align with their personal values.

The benefits of index funds and ETFs extend beyond low costs and broad exposure. These investments also offer a high degree of transparency, as they are designed to match the holdings of their underlying index, making it easy for investors to know what they own. For single women who may not have time to research individual stocks or manage a complex portfolio, index funds and ETFs provide a simple yet effective way to grow wealth. By selecting funds that track well-established indexes, investors gain exposure to a diverse range of companies, reducing the risks of poor performance by any single company. This diversified approach is particularly valuable for those focused on building a reliable nest egg for retirement. Over time, the consistent growth and low fees associated with index funds and ETFs make them a powerful addition to a retirement strategy, providing both stability and growth potential.

Building a portfolio with a mix of index funds and ETFs also allows for customizable risk levels and targeted exposure to preferred markets. For instance, a young professional might allocate more heavily to stock-based ETFs to maximize growth, while someone closer to retirement might choose bond-focused ETFs to enhance stability and income. This flexibility supports a retirement strategy that evolves with life changes, accommodating shifts in income, financial goals, and risk tolerance. By incorporating index funds and ETFs, single women can create a robust, low-maintenance portfolio that positions them for long-term financial independence.

Understanding Socially Responsible Investing

Socially responsible investing (SRI) allows individuals to align their financial decisions with their personal values, an approach that is increasingly popular among single women seeking to make a positive impact through their investments. SRI involves selecting companies and funds based on environmental, social, and governance (ESG) criteria, ensuring that investments reflect a commitment to sustainable and ethical practices. Many SRI funds avoid investing in industries that are considered harmful, such as fossil fuels, tobacco, or weapons, and instead focus on companies promoting renewable energy, social equality, and corporate accountability. For investors interested in fostering positive change while building wealth, socially responsible investing offers a way to support causes they care about while also aiming for strong financial returns.

The appeal of SRI lies in its dual focus on profit and purpose. By investing in companies that prioritize ESG principles, investors can support practices that benefit society and the environment. This focus is particularly relevant as awareness of issues such as climate change, social justice, and corporate ethics continues to grow. Socially responsible funds often include companies with strong environmental policies, fair labor practices, and transparent corporate governance, creating a portfolio that reflects ethical values. For single women who prioritize impact as much as profit, SRI provides a pathway to grow their retirement funds while contributing to a more equitable and sustainable world. Over the past decade, SRI funds have shown competitive performance, dispelling the notion that socially conscious investing requires sacrificing returns.

Investing in SRI can be approached through various vehicles, including ESG-focused mutual funds, ETFs, and individual stocks. Many financial institutions offer SRI funds that cater to different themes, such as clean energy, gender equality, or community development, enabling investors to choose causes they are passionate about. ESG-focused ETFs provide a convenient, diversified option that supports socially responsible goals while maintaining low fees. This accessibility has made SRI a practical option for investors of all experience levels, including those just beginning to build a retirement portfolio. As more companies recognize the importance of ESG principles, SRI portfolios are becoming increasingly diversified, covering a wide array of sectors and industries that contribute to long-term growth and stability.

For single women focused on retirement, SRI offers a way to invest with confidence, knowing that their financial contributions support values that resonate with them personally. Many SRI funds actively engage with the companies they invest in, pushing for transparency, improved labor practices, and stronger environmental policies. This proactive approach not only holds companies accountable but also encourages positive change within industries. As these funds become more common and continue to perform well, socially responsible investing stands as a powerful way to contribute to meaningful causes while building a secure retirement. For those who believe in investing for both personal gain and social good, SRI offers a compelling strategy that integrates financial growth with ethical impact. By incorporating SRI principles into their portfolios, single women can build wealth while knowing their investments are aligned with their values and contributing to a more positive global future.

Navigating Retirement Accounts

Planning for retirement involves a variety of financial tools, among which dedicated retirement accounts are essential. These accounts, like 401(k)s, IRAs, and Roth IRAs, are designed to encourage savings by offering tax advantages that help maximize contributions and grow investments. For single women, understanding these options is crucial for building a secure financial future, as these accounts provide unique benefits that cater to different financial situations, tax circumstances, and long-term goals. Choosing the right retirement account and knowing how to maximize its potential can significantly impact retirement readiness and ensure a steady income stream during retirement years. Each account has distinct tax implications, eligibility criteria, and growth potential, making it important to assess one's financial needs and objectives when deciding which account or combination of accounts will offer the most benefits.

Knowing how to optimize contributions to these accounts, especially if employer-matching contributions are available, can enhance long-term wealth accumulation. Employer-sponsored retirement accounts like 401(k)s and 403(b)s are popular choices, as they often come with matching contributions, allowing employees to increase their retirement savings without extra personal investment. For those without access to employer-sponsored plans, IRAs and Roth IRAs offer flexibility and tax advantages, though contribution limits and eligibility are factors to consider. By carefully assessing income level, tax bracket, and projected retirement needs, single women can select accounts that offer the best balance of tax savings, growth potential, and flexibility, creating a well-rounded approach to long-term financial security.

401(k)s, IRAs, and Roth IRAs: Choosing the Right Account

Selecting the right retirement account begins with understanding the three most common types—401(k)s, IRAs, and Roth IRAs—and the specific advantages each offers. A 401(k) is an employer-sponsored retirement plan, allowing employees to contribute a portion of their pre-tax income, which reduces taxable income in the present. This tax-deferred approach means that contributions and investment earnings are only taxed upon withdrawal, typically during retirement when individuals may be in a lower tax bracket. Additionally, employers often match a percentage of employee contributions, effectively providing "free" money that increases the total retirement savings. For single women with access to employer-sponsored plans, maximizing these contributions is an excellent strategy for building retirement wealth. Contribution limits for 401(k)s are generally higher than for IRAs, enabling employees to save more annually, with catch-up contributions available for those aged 50 and older.

For those who do not have access to a 401(k) or who wish to save beyond the limits of an employer-sponsored plan, an Individual Retirement Account (IRA) is a valuable option. Traditional IRAs offer a tax-deferred growth model, similar to a 401(k), where contributions may be tax-deductible depending on income level and whether the individual has access to another retirement plan. Roth IRAs, on the other hand, operate with after-tax contributions, meaning the funds grow tax-free and withdrawals during retirement are also tax-free, as long as certain conditions are met. This tax-free growth can be particularly beneficial for those who expect to be in a higher tax bracket during retirement or who value flexibility, as Roth IRAs have fewer restrictions on withdrawals before retirement age. However, Roth IRA contributions have income eligibility limits, which may restrict high earners from contributing directly.

Considering one's income, tax bracket, and retirement goals is essential when deciding between a traditional IRA and a Roth IRA. Traditional IRAs offer immediate tax benefits through potential deductions on contributions, which can be advantageous for those seeking to lower taxable income in high-income years. This option may appeal to single women who anticipate a lower income in retirement, as it allows them to defer taxes until they are in a lower bracket. Roth IRAs, on the other hand, may be ideal for those who want tax-free income in retirement and anticipate that their future tax bracket will be higher. For those who are eligible, Roth IRAs also provide flexibility, as contributions (but not earnings) can be withdrawn at any time without penalty, making them suitable for those who may need occasional access to funds before retirement.

For single women aiming to optimize their retirement strategy, a combination of these accounts may provide the best balance. For instance, contributing to an employer-sponsored 401(k) up to the match, then directing additional savings to a Roth IRA, allows individuals to benefit from immediate tax savings and long-term tax-free growth. This approach diversifies the tax treatment of retirement income, providing more control over taxable income in retirement. By carefully considering current income, expected future income, and retirement needs, single women can select the most appropriate combination of retirement accounts, tailoring their savings strategy to maximize both growth and tax advantages.

Maximizing Employer Contributions if Available

Employer contributions in 401(k) plans can make a substantial difference in retirement savings, providing a valuable boost that enhances the power of compounding over time. Employer matching contributions are one of the most effective ways to grow retirement savings, as they represent a direct increase in the amount saved without requiring additional personal investment. For instance, an employer may match 50% of employee contributions up to a certain percentage of salary, often around 3-6%. Taking full advantage of this match is critical, as failing to contribute enough to receive the full match effectively leaves "free" money on the table. By contributing at least enough to receive the full employer match, single women can maximize the benefits of their 401(k) plan and significantly enhance their retirement savings.

Employer contributions are particularly valuable because they grow on a tax-deferred basis, allowing both the employee's and employer's contributions to compound over time. This long-term compounding effect can lead to significant wealth accumulation, especially when contributions are consistent. Even small contributions matched by an employer can grow substantially over the course of a career, creating a solid foundation for retirement. For single women who may have fewer income sources to rely on in retirement, maximizing employer-matched contributions is a straightforward and effective way to build a robust retirement fund. Regularly reviewing contribution levels, especially after salary increases, ensures that contributions remain at the necessary level to capture the full employer match and optimize retirement savings.

Another advantage of employer-sponsored 401(k) plans is the ability to make catch-up contributions for those aged 50 and older. Catch-up contributions allow individuals to increase their annual 401(k) contributions beyond the standard limit, providing an opportunity to accelerate savings in the years leading up to retirement. This can be especially valuable for single women who may need to prioritize building a retirement fund later in life due to career breaks or other financial commitments earlier on. By taking advantage of catch-up contributions, individuals can boost their savings during high-earning years, making up for potential shortfalls in retirement preparation. When combined with employer matching, catch-up contributions can further enhance retirement readiness, providing a greater level of financial security and flexibility in retirement.

For those without access to employer-sponsored plans, alternative savings strategies should be explored to achieve similar growth. In these cases, contributing to an IRA or Roth IRA becomes even more important, as these accounts offer tax advantages that promote long-term savings. By maximizing contributions to individual retirement accounts and exploring additional options such as taxable investment accounts, single women can still build a solid retirement fund even without employer support. This disciplined approach to saving, with a focus on regular contributions and tax-advantaged growth, provides a path to financial independence and a secure retirement.

Traditional vs. Roth IRAs: Which is Best for Your Needs?

Deciding between a traditional and Roth IRA requires a clear understanding of the tax implications, eligibility requirements, and long-term goals associated with each account. Traditional IRAs offer the advantage of tax-deferred growth, which can be appealing to those who seek to reduce taxable income during high-earning years. Contributions to a traditional IRA may be tax-deductible, depending on income level and access to other retirement plans, providing immediate tax savings. This feature makes traditional IRAs suitable for those looking to minimize tax obligations in the present and defer them until retirement, when income—and, potentially, tax rates—may be lower. During retirement, withdrawals from traditional IRAs are taxed as ordinary income, which can affect taxable income in retirement and may lead to taxes on Social Security benefits and other income sources.

A Roth IRA, on the other hand, offers tax-free growth and tax-free withdrawals, as contributions are made with after-tax dollars. This approach is advantageous for those who anticipate being in a higher tax bracket during retirement or who want to avoid future tax liability on their retirement income. Roth IRAs also provide greater flexibility than traditional IRAs, as contributions (but not earnings) can be withdrawn at any time without penalty. This feature can be particularly useful for single women who may need occasional access to funds for emergencies or other financial needs before retirement age. Roth IRAs are also not subject to required minimum distributions (RMDs) during the account holder's lifetime, allowing funds to grow for as long as needed, which can be a strategic advantage for those who wish to leave a legacy or have additional income in later retirement.

Eligibility for Roth IRA contributions is based on income level, which may limit high earners' ability to contribute directly. However, those ineligible for direct contributions to a Roth IRA can consider a "backdoor" conversion by contributing to a traditional IRA and then converting those funds to a Roth IRA, though this process involves careful tax planning. For individuals with varying income levels over time, using both a traditional and Roth IRA can create a diversified tax strategy, allowing for tax-deferred savings and tax-free growth. This balanced approach gives retirees greater control over taxable income in retirement, as they can draw from both taxable and tax-free sources as needed.

Ultimately, the choice between a traditional and Roth IRA depends on individual circumstances, projected future income, and retirement goals. For single women who are uncertain about their future tax situation, contributing to both accounts can provide flexibility and tax diversification, allowing them to adapt their withdrawal strategy to maximize tax efficiency in retirement. By assessing current tax needs, income stability, and long-term objectives, single women can make informed choices that will support financial security throughout retirement.

Part 3: Safeguarding Your Future

Insurance Essentials for Single Women

Planning for retirement is not solely about saving and investing; comprehensive insurance coverage is also essential. For single women, insurance provides security in the face of unforeseen events, protecting against potentially devastating costs associated with health issues, long-term care needs, or loss of income. Insurance offers financial support when dealing with unexpected life changes, and selecting the right policies can be particularly impactful for those without a partner to rely on for shared income or caregiving. With careful consideration of health insurance, long-term care insurance, life insurance, and disability insurance, single women can build a safety net that ensures their financial stability remains intact throughout retirement and in the face of any challenges.

A solid insurance plan should be designed to match individual needs and financial circumstances. Health insurance provides critical coverage for medical expenses, which can be a significant burden in retirement, while Medicare fills many gaps but may not cover all health-related costs. Long-term care insurance, though not necessary for everyone, can be a valuable option for those concerned about long-term assisted living expenses. Disability insurance helps protect income before retirement, and life insurance can offer added financial protection for loved ones or cover final expenses. By understanding and carefully selecting these essential insurance options, single women can approach retirement with confidence, knowing they are prepared for the unexpected.

Health Insurance and Medicare: Planning for Healthcare in Retirement

Healthcare expenses can be one of the most significant financial challenges during retirement, especially as medical needs often increase with age. Health insurance coverage, therefore, is a vital part of retirement planning. Before age 65, single women need to consider how to maintain adequate health insurance coverage, whether through employer-sponsored plans, private insurance, or the Affordable Care Act marketplace. Health insurance not only covers routine medical expenses but also provides a financial buffer for unexpected medical emergencies. For those approaching retirement, budgeting for health insurance premiums and understanding policy options is essential to avoid financial strain. Women planning to retire early must be particularly vigilant, as they may need to secure individual health insurance coverage until they are eligible for Medicare at age 65. Health Savings Accounts (HSAs) can also be beneficial for covering health-related expenses in retirement, offering tax advantages when used for qualifying medical expenses and providing a supplemental healthcare fund as retirement approaches.

Once an individual reaches 65, Medicare becomes the primary source of health insurance, and understanding its structure is crucial for making informed decisions. Medicare is divided into parts, each covering specific healthcare needs. Medicare Part A covers hospital stays, skilled nursing facilities, and hospice care, and is typically premium-free for those who have worked and paid Medicare taxes. However, out-of-pocket costs, such as deductibles and coinsurance, still apply, and Medicare Part A does not cover all medical needs. Medicare Part B covers doctor visits, outpatient services, and preventive care, requiring a monthly premium based on income level. Together, Parts A and B make up "Original Medicare," but this coverage may not be sufficient for those with additional healthcare needs, leading many retirees to consider supplemental insurance options, known as Medigap, or Medicare Advantage plans.

Medicare Advantage (Part C) plans offer a comprehensive alternative to Original Medicare by bundling Parts A, B, and often Part D, which covers prescription drugs, into a single plan provided by private insurers. These plans may also include benefits not covered by Original Medicare, such as dental, vision, and hearing services. However, Medicare Advantage plans have network restrictions and may require referrals for specialist care, so assessing personal healthcare needs and preferences is essential when choosing between Original Medicare and Medicare Advantage. For those sticking with Original Medicare, enrolling in a Part D plan for prescription drug coverage is advisable, as medication costs can quickly add up, especially for those managing chronic conditions. Part D plans have their own monthly premiums and out-of-pocket costs, making it important to review available options based on medications and healthcare needs.

Medigap policies, or Medicare Supplement Insurance, are designed to help cover out-of-pocket costs not covered by Original Medicare, including copayments, coinsurance, and deductibles. While Medigap plans do not cover prescription drugs, they provide more predictable healthcare expenses and offer greater flexibility in choosing providers. Medigap can be a valuable option for single women who prefer the freedom to select healthcare providers without network restrictions, though these plans generally come with higher premiums. For those considering Medigap, it is essential to purchase coverage during the Medigap open enrollment period, as medical underwriting may make it more difficult to qualify or increase premiums after this period. By thoroughly researching and selecting the appropriate Medicare coverage, single women can ensure they have the medical support needed without incurring overwhelming costs in retirement.

Long-Term Care Insurance: Do You Need It?

Long-term care insurance (LTCI) is designed to cover the expenses associated with extended care needs, such as assistance with daily living activities or custodial care in nursing homes, assisted living facilities, or even at home. As individuals age, the likelihood of requiring long-term care increases, and the associated costs can quickly deplete retirement savings. For single women who may not have a spouse or children to assist with caregiving, planning for potential long-term care needs is crucial to avoid financial hardship. Long-term care insurance offers a financial safety net that covers these costs, providing greater independence and reducing the need to rely on loved ones or government assistance.

The decision to purchase long-term care insurance depends on several factors, including health, family medical history, income, and retirement savings. Long-term care is not covered by Medicare, except for limited skilled nursing care following a hospital stay, leaving many people unprepared for the significant costs of extended care. Medicaid, a state and federal program, does cover long-term care, but it requires individuals to spend down their assets to qualify, which can be financially limiting. Long-term care insurance allows single women to retain control over their assets while ensuring they have access to quality care options.

Long-term care insurance premiums can be expensive, and policyholders may never need to use the benefits, but the security it provides can be invaluable for those who prioritize having choices and control over their care. Premiums are generally lower when policies are purchased at a younger age, so evaluating the potential costs and benefits of long-term care insurance before reaching retirement is advisable. Policies vary in terms of coverage duration, daily benefit limits, and elimination periods (the waiting period before benefits begin), so it's important to select a policy that aligns with personal needs and financial resources. Additionally, hybrid insurance products, such as life insurance policies with long-term care riders, have become increasingly popular, as they provide a death benefit if long-term care is never needed.

For single women considering long-term care insurance, weighing the premiums against the potential costs of care is essential. Some may decide to self-fund long-term care expenses by allocating savings specifically for this purpose, particularly if they have significant assets. However, for those concerned about preserving assets or accessing high-quality care, long-term care insurance can offer peace of mind and flexibility. By understanding long-term care insurance options, single women can proactively prepare for future care needs and ensure they maintain financial stability and dignity in their later years.

Life and Disability Insurance: Planning for the Unexpected

Life and disability insurance play vital roles in providing financial security for single women, particularly those who may have dependents or who wish to safeguard their financial independence. Life insurance offers a way to provide for loved ones or cover final expenses, while disability insurance protects against loss of income due to illness or injury, which can be particularly impactful for those without a second household income. For single women who are actively working and rely on their income to meet financial obligations, both life and disability insurance can be valuable investments, shielding against scenarios that could otherwise disrupt financial stability.

Life insurance is generally used to replace lost income or to provide a financial benefit to dependents or designated beneficiaries. For single women, life insurance may not seem as essential if there are no dependents, but it can still serve practical purposes. A life insurance policy can be used to cover funeral expenses, pay off any remaining debts, or leave a legacy for a charitable cause. For those who wish to protect family members from financial burdens, a small life insurance policy can provide peace of mind. Term life insurance is often the most affordable option, covering a specific period, such as until retirement age, and can offer significant coverage at lower premiums compared to permanent life insurance policies.

Disability insurance, however, is perhaps even more critical for single women, as it replaces a portion of income if they are unable to work due to injury or illness. Unlike life insurance, disability insurance protects an individual's ability to earn income, which is particularly important for single women who are solely responsible for their own financial well-being. Short-term disability insurance typically covers income for up to six months, while long-term disability insurance can provide benefits for several years or until retirement age. Employer-sponsored plans may offer some level of disability insurance, but it is often advisable to supplement this coverage with an individual policy that aligns with personal income and needs. Ensuring adequate disability insurance means that in the event of a serious health condition, a single woman can maintain financial stability, avoiding the need to rely on savings or incur debt to cover living expenses.

In choosing life and disability insurance policies, considering factors such as policy terms, benefit amounts, and premium costs is essential. For life insurance, a term policy with sufficient coverage to handle any outstanding debts and final expenses is often suitable. For disability insurance, selecting a policy that provides at least 60-70% of pre-disability income is typically recommended to maintain a comparable standard of living. These insurance choices represent a proactive approach to protecting one's financial future, as they mitigate the risk of losing income or leaving financial burdens behind. By incorporating life and disability insurance into a retirement strategy, single women can safeguard their financial independence and ensure they are prepared for any circumstances life may bring.

Estate Planning for the Solo Retiree

Estate planning is a vital process that allows single retirees to organize their assets, specify their healthcare preferences, and determine who will manage their affairs when they are no longer able to do so. While some may view estate planning as something relevant only for those with considerable wealth, it is essential for anyone who wants to control the distribution of their assets and protect their interests. For single individuals without a spouse to automatically inherit assets or manage decisions, taking the time to outline a detailed estate plan becomes even more critical. Without proper estate planning, assets may be subject to probate, a lengthy and potentially costly process, and healthcare decisions may be made by others who may not understand or respect personal preferences. This planning can ensure that assets are managed and distributed according to individual wishes, providing peace of mind and safeguarding both financial and healthcare-related decisions.

For solo retirees, estate planning offers an opportunity to address various critical aspects, including the distribution of personal property, charitable giving, and even pet care provisions. The process often involves creating documents such as wills, durable powers of attorney, and advanced healthcare directives. These documents together ensure that designated individuals can manage both financial and medical decisions if one becomes incapacitated or passes away. Establishing a solid estate plan enables single retirees to address the potential challenges associated with aging and to make proactive decisions about asset distribution. Whether the goal is to leave assets to family members, support charitable organizations, or assign a trusted individual to make healthcare decisions, a comprehensive estate plan empowers solo retirees to protect their legacy and personal wishes.

Creating a Will and Power of Attorney

A will is one of the most fundamental estate planning tools, allowing individuals to dictate how their assets will be distributed upon their death. For single retirees, creating a will ensures that personal assets, including real estate, savings, investments, and sentimental belongings, are given to the chosen beneficiaries, rather than being left to state law, which may otherwise determine the distribution. In the absence of a spouse, it is particularly important to have a clear, legally recognized document that conveys these wishes. Without a will, a person's estate is subject to intestate succession laws, which may result in assets being distributed in ways that do not align with personal intentions. Creating a will not only clarifies asset distribution but can also designate an executor, an individual responsible for carrying out these wishes, who can be someone trusted to manage financial affairs competently.

Alongside a will, establishing a durable power of attorney (POA) is essential for managing financial and legal matters in the event of incapacity. A durable POA authorizes a designated person to act on behalf of an individual in managing assets, paying bills, handling taxes, and conducting other necessary financial transactions if the individual becomes unable to make decisions. This arrangement is crucial for single retirees who may not have a spouse to take over these responsibilities. Choosing the right person to act as a power of attorney requires careful consideration, as this individual will have control over financial decisions and, in some cases, even sell or transfer assets if needed. This selected individual should ideally be someone trustworthy, financially responsible, and capable of making informed decisions on behalf of the retiree. For those without a close family member or friend who is suitable, professional fiduciaries, such as attorneys or financial advisors, can be appointed.

In addition to a financial POA, a healthcare power of attorney allows an individual to name someone to make healthcare decisions if they are no longer able to do so. For single retirees, a healthcare POA ensures that medical treatments, long-term care decisions, and end-of-life preferences are respected and handled by someone who understands personal wishes. Healthcare powers of attorney are often paired with an advance healthcare directive or living will, which provides specific instructions on medical treatments that are acceptable or unacceptable, such as resuscitation or life support. By preparing both a financial and healthcare POA, single retirees can be assured that trusted individuals are in place to act in their best interests should they be unable to communicate or make decisions on their own.

Naming Beneficiaries and Choosing a Guardian

Designating beneficiaries is another essential aspect of estate planning, as it specifies who will inherit various financial accounts, life insurance policies, and retirement savings. Single retirees should regularly review and update their beneficiary designations, as these take precedence over any instructions in a will. Many assets, such as IRAs, 401(k)s, and life insurance policies, allow the account holder to name beneficiaries directly on the account, bypassing the probate process. Naming beneficiaries is straightforward but requires attention to detail; failing to update beneficiaries or neglecting to specify contingent beneficiaries can lead to unintended consequences. For example, if a primary beneficiary predeceases the retiree and no contingent beneficiary is named, the asset may go through probate. By keeping beneficiary designations current, single retirees ensure that these assets are passed directly to the intended individuals without delays.

For retirees who have minor children, naming a guardian is a critical part of the estate plan. Although not every solo retiree will have minor dependents, those who do must consider who will care for their children in the event of their passing. A guardian is a legally designated individual who assumes responsibility for the child's well-being, including housing, education, and healthcare. Choosing a guardian is a deeply personal decision, one that should consider the guardian's values, lifestyle, financial stability, and willingness to care for the child. Without a designated guardian in a will, the decision may be left to the court, which may not always align with parental intentions. Even if an ideal guardian is evident, it is wise to discuss this role with them in advance, ensuring they are prepared and willing to assume the responsibility.

In addition to financial beneficiaries and guardians, retirees may wish to consider pet care provisions. Many people have pets they care deeply about and would like to see them well looked after should they pass away. Some estate plans include pet trusts, which set aside funds specifically for the care of pets, or at least designate a trusted individual as the pet's caretaker. Given that pets are legally considered property, they cannot inherit money directly, so a pet trust is a viable option for ensuring they receive the care they need. Designating both human and animal beneficiaries and caretakers provides peace of mind that loved ones—whether children, pets, or close friends—are supported and protected.

Trusts, Executors, and Other Estate Planning Tools

Trusts are valuable estate planning tools that allow for the transfer of assets while avoiding probate, providing greater privacy and control over how assets are distributed. A trust can be particularly advantageous for single retirees with considerable assets or specific intentions for asset distribution. Unlike a will, which becomes part of the public record, trusts remain private, providing discretion over financial matters. There are various types of trusts available, including revocable living trusts, which allow the grantor to retain control over assets and amend the trust as needed, and irrevocable trusts, which cannot be altered once established but offer benefits such as protection from creditors and potential tax advantages. For solo retirees who wish to ensure seamless asset transfer, reduce estate taxes, or protect assets from potential long-term care costs, establishing a trust can be a prudent decision.

In addition to setting up a trust, appointing an executor to manage the estate is a crucial part of estate planning. The executor, also known as a personal representative, is responsible for administering the estate, ensuring that debts and taxes are paid, and distributing assets according to the terms of the will or trust. For single retirees, selecting a reliable and trustworthy executor is essential, as this individual will be tasked with settling final affairs. Executors may be family members, friends, or professional fiduciaries, and the choice should be based on the complexity of the estate and the skills required to manage it. If the estate includes real estate, business interests, or significant financial assets, an experienced professional executor may be beneficial.

Additional estate planning tools include advanced directives, such as living wills, and other healthcare documents, which specify end-of-life care preferences. Living wills provide instructions on medical interventions in case of terminal illness or permanent incapacity, and they work alongside healthcare powers of attorney to ensure that healthcare wishes are followed. Advanced directives can relieve family members or close friends of the burden of making difficult medical decisions, providing clear guidance on personal preferences. For single retirees, these documents represent a powerful means of maintaining control over healthcare decisions and reducing the stress on loved ones during challenging times.

Estate planning also involves making decisions about digital assets, which may include online accounts, social media profiles, digital subscriptions, and intellectual property. Designating a digital executor or including digital asset instructions in the estate plan ensures that these accounts are properly managed or closed, reducing the risk of identity theft and protecting personal information. Digital assets can hold sentimental or financial value, so including them in an estate plan safeguards these assets as part of a comprehensive plan.

By carefully utilizing estate planning tools such as trusts, executors, advanced directives, and digital asset instructions, solo retirees can build an estate plan that respects their wishes and simplifies the process for those managing their affairs. These tools provide flexibility and protection, allowing for smooth asset distribution, tax reduction, and control over healthcare decisions. A well-rounded estate plan is essential for single retirees, offering security, clarity, and peace of mind in their financial, healthcare, and personal affairs.

Managing Social Security and Other Benefits

Effectively managing Social Security and other government benefits is crucial for single women planning for a secure retirement. Social Security serves as a core component of retirement income for many, and for single women in particular, it can represent a significant part of financial stability later in life. Because single women do not have a spouse's income or benefits to rely on, they must approach Social Security with strategic planning to maximize its value. Additionally, other government programs, such as Supplemental Security Income (SSI) and various assistance programs, can play important roles in supplementing income and covering healthcare or long-term care needs. Understanding the complexities of these programs, from timing considerations to potential supplemental resources, can help single women craft a retirement strategy that optimally leverages all available benefits.

Navigating Social Security and government assistance programs often involves understanding eligibility requirements, benefit calculations, and strategies for timing claims to maximize income. With Social Security, single women face unique considerations; they cannot split or combine benefits with a spouse, and they may need to weigh the benefits of delaying Social Security to increase monthly income versus claiming earlier for immediate financial support. Additionally, exploring options for SSI and other government aid may be necessary to ensure comprehensive support in retirement. By examining Social Security and related programs in depth, single women can make informed decisions that increase their financial security, helping them better handle the challenges of a solo retirement.

Understanding Social Security: Timing and Strategies

Social Security retirement benefits play a central role in retirement planning, especially for individuals who may not have substantial personal savings or other sources of income. For single women, Social Security often represents a reliable income stream that is adjusted annually for inflation, providing some degree of protection against rising living costs. However, choosing when to claim benefits can have a significant impact on the amount received each month. Understanding how Social Security benefits are calculated and considering strategies for optimizing these benefits can greatly improve financial stability in retirement.

Social Security retirement benefits are calculated based on an individual's highest 35 years of earnings, and the monthly benefit amount depends on the age at which a person begins to claim. While benefits can be claimed as early as age 62, doing so results in a reduction, as monthly amounts are adjusted downward to account for the extended duration over which payments are expected to be received. Conversely, delaying Social Security benefits past the full retirement age (which varies depending on the birth year) increases the monthly payout, with the maximum benefit achieved if one waits until age 70 to start receiving benefits. This increase, known as delayed retirement credits, can add up to approximately 8 percent per year, offering a substantial boost to monthly income.

For single women, deciding when to claim Social Security benefits requires careful consideration of factors such as life expectancy, current health, and immediate financial needs. Those in good health who expect to live longer may benefit from delaying benefits to maximize monthly income over the long term. Conversely, individuals who may face health concerns or immediate financial needs may consider claiming benefits earlier to access income sooner. Because single women do not have a spouse's Social Security benefits to supplement their own, the decision on timing can have an outsized impact on long-term financial security. Many financial planners recommend running detailed projections to compare the cumulative value of early versus delayed benefits, taking into account individual health and lifestyle.

There are also strategies to consider, such as the restricted application strategy for certain beneficiaries born before 1954, allowing them to receive benefits based on an ex-spouse's earnings record while delaying their own benefits. While this option is limited to specific cases, understanding the various nuances of Social Security rules can make a meaningful difference. Additionally, coordinating Social Security benefits with other retirement income sources, such as pensions or investment withdrawals, is essential for ensuring steady income and managing potential tax implications.

Maximizing Benefits as a Single Woman

Single women face unique challenges in maximizing Social Security benefits, as they are solely dependent on their own earnings record without a spouse's benefits to bolster income. However, single women who have been married for at least ten years may qualify for benefits based on an ex-spouse's earnings, which can provide an alternative source of Social Security income in retirement. For those eligible, spousal benefits can amount to up to 50 percent of an ex-spouse's benefit, and the former spouse does not need to be aware or approve of the application. This benefit can be a lifeline for women whose work history might not generate a robust Social Security payment, offering an additional layer of financial security.

For those who do not qualify for spousal or ex-spousal benefits, the focus shifts to maximizing the benefits derived from personal earnings. One way to increase Social Security payments is to ensure a full 35-year work history, as benefits are calculated based on the highest-earning 35 years. If there are fewer than 35 years of recorded earnings, Social Security averages in zero-earning years, which can significantly lower the monthly benefit. For women who have taken time off from the workforce, whether to raise children or care for family members, working additional years to replace low or zero-earning years can help increase the monthly benefit. Additionally, aiming to earn at least the Social Security taxable maximum (currently set at a certain amount each year) can maximize the benefits base and increase the average benefit amount over time.

Another essential consideration is the coordination of Social Security with other income sources, as certain income levels can make Social Security benefits taxable. For single retirees with moderate to high retirement income, a portion of Social Security benefits may become subject to federal taxes if combined income exceeds specific thresholds. Strategic income withdrawals from other retirement accounts can help manage taxable income and reduce the tax burden on Social Security benefits. By being aware of these thresholds and planning withdrawals accordingly, single women can potentially reduce overall tax liability, retaining more of their Social Security income for essential expenses and quality of life in retirement.

For single women with longer life expectancies, which is common, planning for Social Security's longevity is also vital. Monthly income increases with inflation adjustments, and choosing the right time to claim benefits can mean receiving more over a lifetime. Single women can benefit greatly from financial planning support or tools that provide a comprehensive analysis of various claiming strategies. Calculating break-even points, understanding survivor benefits, and accounting for healthcare expenses can help single women make well-informed decisions regarding Social Security, maximizing the financial benefit and ensuring better security for the future.

Supplemental Security Income and Other Government Assistance

While Social Security is a primary retirement income source for many, other government assistance programs can serve as crucial supplements, especially for single women who may face additional financial challenges. Supplemental Security Income (SSI) is a needs-based program that provides monthly payments to individuals with limited income and resources who are either disabled, blind, or aged 65 and older. Unlike Social Security retirement benefits, SSI does not require a work history; it is funded by general tax revenues and intended as an additional safety net for those who meet financial eligibility criteria. For single women with limited savings or retirement income, SSI can be an essential supplement, helping to cover basic expenses and providing a modest level of income security.

To qualify for SSI, applicants must meet strict income and asset limits, which vary slightly by state, as some states provide additional SSI benefits. Understanding these limits and ensuring that finances align with eligibility requirements can open up this additional source of income. SSI can also work alongside other benefits, including Medicaid, which provides health insurance to low-income individuals. For single women who may be managing healthcare costs on a fixed income, the combination of SSI and Medicaid can make healthcare and long-term care services more affordable and accessible.

In addition to SSI, there are other forms of government assistance that can support retirement goals. Programs like the Supplemental Nutrition Assistance Program (SNAP) provide food assistance to individuals with low income, and the Low-Income Home Energy Assistance Program (LIHEAP) helps cover heating and cooling expenses. Both of these programs reduce the financial strain on monthly budgets, allowing more of a retiree's Social Security or SSI income to be used for other needs. Furthermore, there are property tax relief programs and senior discount programs available in certain states, which can help single women reduce living costs and stretch their retirement income further.

Planning for government assistance involves understanding eligibility requirements, the application process, and the coordination of benefits to optimize support. For example, applicants may need to provide documentation of their income, assets, and medical needs. Meeting these requirements can involve gathering records of Social Security statements, bank accounts, investment accounts, and health conditions. Navigating government assistance programs can be complex, but the benefits can greatly relieve financial pressure, allowing single women to enjoy a higher quality of life in retirement.

For single women, combining Social Security, SSI, and other government assistance programs with personal savings and investments can form a robust financial plan, enabling a more comfortable and secure retirement. The right combination of these benefits can help cover essential expenses, address healthcare needs, and create a stable foundation for the years ahead. By thoughtfully managing these resources and understanding the benefits available, single women can design a retirement strategy that provides both peace of mind and financial freedom.

Part 4: Creating a Lifestyle for a Fulfilling Retirement

Planning Your Ideal Retirement Lifestyle

Creating an ideal retirement lifestyle is a deeply personal journey, reflecting years of dreams, aspirations, and practical considerations that will shape how retirement unfolds. With newfound freedom from career obligations, retirement offers an opportunity to explore interests, pursue passions, and build meaningful routines that align with individual values and preferences. For many, this stage of life serves as a blank canvas to redefine daily life beyond traditional boundaries, whether it means nurturing long-held hobbies, learning new skills, or dedicating more time to travel and community involvement. Thoughtful planning is essential, allowing individuals to craft a balanced life that sustains happiness, fulfillment, and personal growth over time.

Designing this lifestyle requires considering various factors, from financial capability to health needs, social connections, and even the possibility of relocating to a more suitable environment. Deciding on a lifestyle also involves contemplating the rhythm and energy of one's retirement days: some may envision quiet, reflective days spent in nature, while others see themselves actively involved in vibrant community groups or traveling extensively. Carefully assessing and aligning these aspirations with realistic goals can create a retirement that is as enriching as it is sustainable, promoting wellness and satisfaction. By focusing on what matters most, retirees can embrace this phase of life with a genuine sense of purpose and contentment.

Exploring Retirement Hobbies and Interests

Hobbies and interests provide a powerful way to bring joy, mental stimulation, and personal satisfaction to retirement life. Without the time constraints of a full-time job, retirees are free to dive into activities that spark curiosity and excitement, from long-time passions to entirely new fields. For some, retirement might represent a chance to revisit an old interest, like painting, writing, or gardening, that may have been sidelined by career demands. Others might be drawn to explore unfamiliar areas like learning a new language, mastering a musical instrument, or engaging in volunteer work that contributes to their community.

Creativity, learning, and self-expression can be particularly fulfilling pursuits during retirement, helping to keep the mind active and engaged. Many retirees find that creative activities, like painting, crafting, or writing, provide not only a source of personal enjoyment but also a therapeutic outlet. Others may enjoy intellectual stimulation by taking courses at a local university or participating in online learning programs. Today, the internet offers nearly limitless possibilities for self-paced education, allowing retirees to study a wide variety of topics, from art history to technology, at their own convenience. For those inclined toward technical skills or hobbies, coding, photography, and digital design have become increasingly popular. Engaging in these pursuits can lead to a sense of achievement and progress, adding a rewarding dimension to retirement life.

Physical hobbies are also important for maintaining health and well-being. Many retirees find joy in activities that involve movement, like hiking, dancing, or practicing yoga. Physical activity not only improves health but also releases endorphins, fostering a positive outlook and combating feelings of loneliness or isolation. Group activities, such as joining a walking group or enrolling in fitness classes, provide an additional layer of social interaction, which can be especially valuable for single retirees. Sports like golfing, tennis, or even community-based activities like bowling leagues and bocce clubs offer both exercise and camaraderie.

Travel is another popular interest that many retirees pursue passionately. With the flexibility that retirement brings, travel becomes more feasible, allowing individuals to embark on extended vacations, experience new cultures, and visit family or friends. Whether traveling domestically or internationally, the exploration of new places stimulates curiosity, and those interested in culture, cuisine, or history may find endless inspiration on their journeys. For some, travel might mean exploring national parks, historical landmarks, or embarking on road trips. Others might opt for international destinations, perhaps spending a season in a European city or exploring Asia's rich history and vibrant modernity. Travel organizations often offer special packages tailored to retirees, with affordable rates and group options that provide companionship and security for those exploring new horizons.

Social hobbies, like joining book clubs, participating in local theater productions, or becoming part of a gardening group, enrich retirees' lives by fostering a sense of connection. Regular participation in social activities helps in building relationships and establishing a network of friends who share common interests. Local community centers, libraries, and online groups offer numerous opportunities to participate in these activities, ensuring that retirees remain socially engaged and connected. Overall, finding a combination of hobbies that blend creativity, physicality, and social engagement can lead to a well-rounded and fulfilling retirement experience.

Building a Support Network: Friends, Community, and Social Engagement

A strong social network is essential for mental, emotional, and even physical well-being in retirement. Without the built-in connections of a workplace, retirees often need to proactively establish and maintain a network of friends, family, and community members to keep a robust social life. Social connections help reduce feelings of isolation and create a sense of belonging, which is vital for single retirees who may not have a partner to rely on. Many find fulfillment in forming bonds with people who share common experiences or interests, which can provide both companionship and emotional support.

Community engagement is one effective way to foster these relationships. Volunteering, for instance, offers opportunities to meet new people while contributing to a meaningful cause. Local charities, hospitals, animal shelters, and environmental groups are always in need of dedicated volunteers, making it easy for retirees to get involved. This interaction fosters a sense of purpose, connecting individuals with others who share their values and goals. Similarly, places of worship, civic organizations, and hobby-based clubs provide spaces where retirees can engage with their community, contributing to a feeling of continuity and stability as they navigate this new phase of life.

In addition to in-person connections, retirees can utilize technology to build and maintain friendships. Video calling, social media, and messaging apps allow for frequent interaction with loved ones, even if they live far away. Many older adults are embracing social media as a way to stay updated on friends' and family's lives, share their own experiences, and join online communities dedicated to their interests. Moreover, online groups can provide a way to meet like-minded individuals across the world, expanding one's social network beyond geographical limits. This can be particularly valuable for single women retirees who may enjoy being part of women's groups, travel clubs, or professional networks that offer ongoing camaraderie and a chance to exchange ideas and advice.

For those who prefer more structured social engagement, retirement communities or 55+ residential communities provide built-in social structures where residents can participate in organized activities, classes, and events. These environments often foster close-knit communities where neighbors support each other and enjoy a shared experience of retirement. Many retirement communities also offer amenities like fitness centers, pools, and libraries, giving residents spaces to gather and socialize regularly. Whether through traditional means or modern technology, establishing a supportive network can add joy and stability to retirement, helping individuals feel connected, valued, and engaged in life.

Relocating for Retirement: Domestic and International Options

Relocation during retirement can open up new opportunities for exploration, lifestyle changes, and financial benefits. Many retirees choose to move to locations that offer a lower cost of living, warmer climate, or closer proximity to family members. This decision is often driven by personal preferences as well as practical considerations, such as access to healthcare, living expenses, and the availability of recreational activities. Relocating within one's home country allows retirees to enjoy the comforts of a familiar environment while possibly benefiting from a reduced cost of living, particularly when moving from a more expensive area to a state or city with affordable housing, tax advantages, and lower overall costs.

Popular domestic retirement destinations often include states like Florida, Arizona, and Texas, known for their favorable climates, vibrant retiree communities, and financial perks. These states generally offer a range of retirement-oriented services and communities, making them attractive choices for those seeking an active lifestyle with minimal seasonal disruptions. Small towns in these states, as well as in the Midwest or Mountain regions, also appeal to those who prefer a quieter setting, offering a slower pace and a lower cost of living. Relocation to a rural or suburban area can mean access to larger properties, beautiful natural settings, and a community-focused way of life.

International relocation presents retirees with additional possibilities, often combining adventure with affordability. Many countries have established programs or visas that welcome retirees, making it relatively straightforward to relocate. Countries in Central and South America, such as Costa Rica, Mexico, and Panama, have become popular for their warm climates, affordable living costs, and friendly communities. Southeast Asia also offers appealing retirement destinations, with countries like Thailand, Malaysia, and Vietnam providing high quality of life at a fraction of the cost found in Western nations. In addition to affordability, these locations offer unique cultural experiences, allowing retirees to enjoy new cuisines, traditions, and lifestyles.

For those considering an international move, it is essential to take healthcare, legal requirements, and language barriers into account. Many retirees prioritize access to affordable and reliable healthcare when choosing a location, and some countries even have medical facilities that cater to expatriates. Legal residency requirements, including retirement visas and income thresholds, should also be carefully reviewed before making any decisions. Language is another factor that can affect the ease of integration, with some retirees preferring countries where English is widely spoken, while others embrace the challenge of learning a new language to fully immerse in the local culture.

Moreover, some individuals opt for a "part-time relocation" strategy, spending only part of the year in a new location while maintaining a home base elsewhere. This seasonal relocation approach, often known as being a "snowbird," is common among those who want to enjoy the benefits of a warmer climate or different lifestyle without fully committing to a permanent move. Seasonal relocations offer the best of both worlds:

access to family and familiarity in one place, combined with the adventure and relaxation of another.

Relocating during retirement can enhance one's lifestyle, financial security, and overall satisfaction by aligning living conditions with personal preferences and goals. Whether moving to a warmer state within one's country or exploring new continents, relocation provides a chance to reimagine retirement in an environment that best supports an ideal lifestyle. By carefully researching and planning, retirees can find a location that feels like home, offering all the ingredients for a happy and fulfilling retirement.

Health and Wellness in Retirement

Maintaining health and wellness is essential for enjoying a fulfilling and independent retirement. This stage of life offers the chance to prioritize well-being, allowing individuals to focus on fitness, mental health, and lifestyle choices that support a long and active life. As people age, the importance of consistent routines for both physical and mental health becomes increasingly clear. By prioritizing wellness, retirees can enhance their quality of life, remain self-sufficient, and stay engaged with their communities. Wellness in retirement goes beyond merely preventing illness; it involves cultivating habits and accessing resources that promote vitality, strength, and resilience.

Retirement provides ample opportunities to establish new health-oriented routines, yet it also requires attention to practical considerations like budgeting and available healthcare options. By understanding the unique wellness needs that arise during this phase and taking proactive steps to meet them, retirees can enjoy a life that is both health-focused and financially sustainable. Developing routines that encompass exercise, healthy eating, mental stimulation, and community engagement can ensure a balanced and enjoyable retirement experience. Accessing the right resources, whether locally or online, empowers individuals to maintain their well-being while staying within budget and building a strong support system.

Staying Active: Physical and Mental Health for Longevity

Staying active during retirement is fundamental to maintaining overall health, as physical and mental activity are closely linked to longevity and well-being. For physical health, regular exercise helps preserve mobility, improve cardiovascular health, and strengthen muscles, all of which contribute to maintaining independence and reducing the risk of injury. Activities like walking, swimming, and gentle strength training are especially beneficial for older adults, as they provide a balanced mix of cardiovascular and muscle-building exercises without putting excessive strain on the body. Yoga and Pilates, with their emphasis on flexibility and core strength, are also effective in supporting stability, which is vital for preventing falls and maintaining mobility as people age. Engaging in physical activity regularly can also reduce symptoms associated with chronic conditions such as arthritis, high blood pressure, and osteoporosis, which often become more common in older age.

In addition to physical exercise, mental stimulation plays a significant role in supporting cognitive health. The brain, like any other muscle, benefits from regular use. Mental exercises like reading, puzzles, and learning new skills help keep the brain sharp, improving memory and cognitive function over time. For instance, activities such as learning a new language or playing a musical instrument challenge the brain and improve its ability to adapt and remain resilient against age-related cognitive decline. Participating in social activities is also known to protect mental health, as socializing stimulates the mind and reduces feelings of loneliness or isolation, which are known risk factors for mental health issues in retirement. In addition, spending time with friends, family, or in community groups provides the brain with opportunities to stay engaged in dynamic, enjoyable conversations and shared experiences.

Finding activities that combine both physical and mental engagement can be particularly beneficial. For example, dance classes or team sports like tennis offer cardiovascular benefits and strengthen muscles, while also requiring coordination, memorization, and quick thinking. Group fitness classes can also be a great choice, as they foster social connections and add an enjoyable element to exercise routines. Even solitary pursuits like gardening or painting have been shown to positively impact mental well-being, providing both physical movement and creative expression. Gardening, for example, involves physical activity as well as planning and decision-making, while creating art engages both fine motor skills and cognitive processes. By focusing on both physical and mental activities, retirees can create a balanced lifestyle that supports health and promotes enjoyment of each day.

Nutrition and Healthy Living on a Retirement Budget

Good nutrition is a cornerstone of health and well-being, but managing a nutritious diet on a retirement budget requires a careful approach. Prioritizing whole foods such as vegetables, fruits, lean proteins, and whole grains can create a diet that supports energy, muscle health, and mental clarity. Planning meals and creating a grocery list can be an effective way to control spending while ensuring that each meal includes essential nutrients. Foods rich in calcium, vitamin D, and omega-3 fatty acids, for instance, are particularly important for maintaining bone and brain health, while antioxidants found in berries, leafy greens, and certain nuts support overall immune function. By choosing nutrient-dense foods, retirees can make the most out of their grocery budget while addressing specific dietary needs that come with age.

Shopping for nutritious foods on a budget often involves selecting seasonal produce, which is generally more affordable and offers higher nutrient content. Local farmers' markets can be an affordable source for fresh fruits and vegetables, and many communities also offer co-op programs that provide members with regular access to seasonal produce at a lower cost. Cooking at home rather than dining out or relying on pre-packaged foods can also save money while enabling control over the ingredients and portion sizes in each meal. Meal planning is another effective strategy, allowing for the preparation of multiple servings at once, which can then be stored and used throughout the week. By preparing meals in advance, individuals can reduce food waste, save time, and maintain a consistent supply of healthy options without the need for frequent grocery trips.

Eating well also involves paying attention to portion sizes, which can contribute to maintaining a healthy weight and managing chronic health conditions. Smaller, more frequent meals may help regulate blood sugar levels and energy throughout the day. For retirees who need to reduce their sodium or sugar intake, reading labels carefully and choosing whole foods over processed options can make a substantial difference in health outcomes. Many foods marketed toward older adults are specifically designed to meet these dietary needs, but it is important to evaluate their actual nutritional value and cost. Simple, nutrient-dense foods like oatmeal, eggs, legumes, and canned fish often provide the same benefits at a fraction of the cost.

Those who wish to incorporate supplements into their diet should do so under the guidance of a healthcare provider, as some supplements can interact with medications or lead to nutrient imbalances if not used carefully. Multivitamins or supplements like calcium, vitamin D, and B12 may be helpful for individuals with specific nutritional needs, though these should be viewed as an addition rather than a replacement for whole foods. With a bit of planning and attention to food choices, it is possible to achieve a well-rounded, nutritious diet that supports healthy aging, even on a limited budget.

Accessing Community and Online Resources for Wellness

Maintaining health and wellness in retirement is often made easier by leveraging the wealth of community and online resources available. Community centers, senior centers, and local health organizations frequently offer fitness classes, health screenings, and wellness programs specifically designed for retirees. These centers provide accessible, affordable opportunities for physical activity, such as tai chi, aerobics, or chair yoga classes, which are particularly beneficial for those seeking low-impact, senior-friendly exercise options. Many also host workshops on nutrition, disease prevention, and mental health, offering essential health education that empowers individuals to take control of their well-being.

Online resources can further expand the options available for maintaining health. Fitness apps and YouTube channels focused on senior fitness provide workout videos that can be completed at home, allowing retirees to stay active without needing to visit a gym. Meditation and mental health apps also offer guided practices that support relaxation, stress management, and mindfulness, which are valuable for overall mental well-being. Many of these apps offer free versions, while others have low-cost subscriptions, making them affordable resources for those on a retirement budget. For retirees looking to engage in community from afar, virtual exercise classes and wellness groups can provide a sense of connection and accountability, helping them stay motivated and engaged with others.

In addition to physical and mental health resources, communities often provide assistance for social engagement, which is equally important for overall wellness. Many cities have programs specifically tailored for retirees, which may include volunteer opportunities, language classes, art workshops, and even book clubs. Libraries and recreational centers are excellent places to find such programs, as they frequently collaborate with local organizations to offer events and activities for retirees. Joining these activities promotes social interaction, adds structure to daily routines, and fosters a sense of belonging.

For those seeking guidance on diet and nutrition, many healthcare providers and dietitians offer online consultations, which can be particularly useful for retirees with specific dietary needs. Community health clinics and nonprofits sometimes provide free or low-cost nutrition counseling, particularly for individuals managing conditions like diabetes or hypertension. Additionally, online platforms host a variety of cooking channels and recipe websites dedicated to nutritious, budget-friendly meals that cater to a wide range of dietary needs. By experimenting with recipes that are nutritious and affordable, retirees can enjoy diverse, delicious meals that support their health goals.

Social media platforms and online forums for retirees provide spaces for individuals to share advice, ask questions, and find support. Many retirees enjoy connecting through interest-based groups, such as fitness, cooking, or travel, which encourage regular interaction and shared experiences. Platforms like Facebook and Reddit offer forums where retirees can discuss wellness strategies, share their progress, and exchange practical tips. These online communities often bring together individuals from all over the world, creating a diverse environment for sharing insights and learning about different wellness approaches.

Ultimately, by taking advantage of the myriad resources available in local communities and online, retirees can craft a personalized wellness plan that suits their unique goals and circumstances. Combining physical, mental, and social health practices allows retirees to build a well-rounded approach to well-being, ensuring that they remain active, engaged, and healthy throughout retirement. The support from both local initiatives and virtual communities can make it easier to maintain these wellness practices consistently, promoting a retirement lifestyle that is enriching, balanced, and deeply fulfilling.

Building Your Retirement Support System

Creating a reliable support system is a vital part of planning a satisfying and secure retirement. For single women, retirement presents unique opportunities to cultivate a network that meets various needs, from practical financial management to emotional support and social engagement. A robust support system ensures that as life changes occur, there are trusted individuals and resources available to offer expertise, guidance, and companionship. Building this network before retirement can be instrumental in establishing a sense of stability and reassurance. Whether through family members, friends, or professionals, a reliable support system can significantly reduce stress, allowing for a smoother transition into retirement and a stronger foundation for a satisfying lifestyle.

Having a network that includes trusted advisors, friends, and community resources provides a well-rounded foundation for retirement. A support system that encompasses multiple facets of life addresses the unique demands that single women may encounter as they age, ensuring their needs are met across the board. From financial advisors and healthcare professionals to social connections that combat isolation, each aspect of this network plays a key role in enriching one's retirement years. Cultivating this support system actively and intentionally can transform retirement into a time of independence and contentment, creating an environment where each day brings a renewed sense of security and fulfillment.

Identifying Trusted Advisors: Financial, Legal, and Medical

A well-prepared retirement is often guided by the wisdom and expertise of trusted advisors in financial, legal, and medical fields. These professionals serve as essential resources, helping to navigate the complexities of retirement planning and to provide peace of mind through informed decision-making. Financial advisors, for example, play a critical role in creating a sustainable retirement plan, offering guidance on investments, budgeting, and risk management. For single women, who may be managing their retirement funds independently, a financial advisor can provide insight into how best to structure portfolios, optimize income streams, and avoid common pitfalls. Finding a financial advisor with experience working with retirees or single women ensures that advice is tailored to fit specific goals and challenges. An advisor who is certified and transparent about fees can be invaluable for long-term financial health and peace of mind.

Legal advisors are equally important, particularly when it comes to safeguarding assets and preparing essential documents like wills, trusts, and power of attorney agreements. Estate planning can be complex, and having a knowledgeable attorney who understands the intricacies of solo retirement is vital for preserving assets and ensuring that wishes are honored. Legal advisors can also offer guidance on how to protect against elder financial abuse, which is a growing concern for older adults. Having these legal measures in place provides reassurance, allowing single women to focus on enjoying their retirement years without unnecessary worry. By establishing a solid legal foundation, retirees can navigate complex situations, like health crises or asset distribution, with greater ease.

Healthcare professionals are another crucial part of a retirement support system, particularly as health needs evolve over time. Establishing relationships with a primary care physician, specialists, and possibly a geriatric care manager allows retirees to approach healthcare proactively. These medical professionals provide regular check-ups, monitor chronic conditions, and offer recommendations for preventive care, all of which contribute to a healthier, more active lifestyle. For women in solo retirement, it's particularly helpful to have trusted medical professionals who understand their health history and can provide continuity of care. A healthcare team that collaborates closely with one another enhances the quality of care, ensuring that potential health concerns are addressed early and with sensitivity to individual circumstances.

Together, this network of financial, legal, and healthcare advisors creates a dependable foundation that empowers single women to make confident decisions about their retirement. As each of these advisors brings specialized knowledge and a commitment to their clients' best interests, they become key pillars of support, capable of guiding retirees through complex decisions. Developing these relationships before retirement helps ensure that these professionals understand personal goals, preferences, and values, enabling them to offer tailored advice and interventions as needed.

Building Emotional Resilience for Retirement as a Solo Woman

Retirement, while offering many benefits, also presents emotional challenges, especially for those retiring alone. Adjusting to a life that is less structured and possibly less socially connected can lead to feelings of loneliness, anxiety, or even loss of purpose. Building emotional resilience helps single women face these challenges with strength, allowing them to fully embrace the possibilities of this stage of life. Resilience is about cultivating mental and emotional flexibility—being able to adapt to change, finding meaning in new circumstances, and maintaining a positive outlook in the face of setbacks. As retirement marks a significant transition, emotional resilience becomes essential for managing the ups and downs of this phase while fostering a sense of purpose and joy.

A proactive approach to emotional well-being can be instrumental in enhancing resilience. Practicing self-care, engaging in regular exercise, and dedicating time to mindfulness or meditation can strengthen mental health and improve overall mood. Many retirees find that journaling or joining a support group provides an outlet for processing emotions and sharing experiences, which can be especially helpful for single women facing unique challenges. Building routines that incorporate both physical and mental wellness activities creates a sense of structure, which can be grounding. Developing hobbies and setting small goals are also powerful ways to maintain a sense of accomplishment and forward momentum, helping to prevent feelings of stagnation that sometimes accompany retirement.

Another essential aspect of resilience is cultivating a sense of independence and self-trust. For solo retirees, becoming comfortable with autonomy and self-sufficiency is key to creating a confident and empowered retirement. This involves acknowledging one's strengths, celebrating personal achievements, and developing a sense of pride in the ability to manage life's complexities alone. Additionally, understanding that it's okay to seek help when needed is important; resilience is not about facing everything alone but about having the wisdom to build a support network that complements personal strengths. By actively focusing on emotional resilience, retirees can enter this chapter with a mindset that fosters fulfillment and self-confidence.

Strategies for Avoiding Loneliness and Building New Friendships

For single retirees, loneliness can pose a significant challenge. Social engagement is not only important for mental well-being but also contributes to physical health, as studies consistently show that strong social connections reduce the risk of health issues. Building new friendships and finding ways to stay socially active allows retirees to create a community of support that enriches their day-to-day lives. To build a circle of meaningful relationships, it can be helpful to explore activities that align with personal interests, such as book clubs, fitness classes, or volunteer organizations. Shared activities naturally facilitate conversation and connection, offering a relaxed setting for meeting like-minded people. Volunteering, in particular, provides a dual benefit of giving back to the community while forming bonds with individuals who share similar values and goals.

Joining local organizations and community centers can also be an excellent way to foster new friendships. Many senior centers and community hubs offer programs tailored to retirees, including classes, social events, and recreational activities. Such environments are designed to support community and encourage interaction, which can be especially comforting for those who are new to retirement and may be seeking a sense of belonging. For women interested in fitness, joining exercise groups like hiking clubs, dance classes, or swimming leagues combines health benefits with socialization, making it easy to bond with others while enjoying a shared interest. Even if socializing doesn't come naturally, these structured group settings provide low-pressure opportunities to connect.

Online platforms and social media have opened new doors for retirees looking to expand their social networks. Virtual communities and interest groups on sites like Facebook or Meetup allow retirees to engage with others from the comfort of home, which can be helpful for those who prefer a gradual approach to socializing. Many retirees also explore online dating or friendship-building platforms specifically designed for older adults, offering a safe way to meet new people who may share similar life stages and interests. Video calls and messaging apps enable individuals to stay connected with distant friends and family, bridging physical distance and allowing for meaningful conversations with loved ones. These tools ensure that single retirees have diverse options to stay socially active and prevent feelings of isolation.

Creating intergenerational friendships is another enriching approach, as it brings a blend of perspectives and energies to social interactions. Younger friends can provide a fresh outlook on life and introduce new activities, while older friends offer camaraderie and understanding of shared life experiences. Many retirees find joy in mentoring or volunteering with youth organizations, which adds meaning to their lives and builds connections with younger generations. Through these bonds, retirees gain a broader sense of community and a feeling of contribution that enhances life's purpose and joy.

By actively pursuing these strategies for social connection, single women in retirement can build a vibrant network of friendships and support. Staying socially engaged not only counters loneliness but also contributes to emotional resilience, helping retirees face life's transitions with grace and positivity. Each connection, whether with friends, family, or community members, enriches the retirement experience, creating a life that is both rewarding and socially fulfilling. Together with a strong support system, these friendships ensure that the retirement years are filled with laughter, companionship, and a renewed sense of connection.

Part 5: Maximizing Your Legacy and Making a Difference

Leaving a Legacy as a Single Woman

Leaving a legacy is a profound and fulfilling way for single women to make a lasting impact on the world. While the concept of legacy is often associated with family and heirs, single women have the unique opportunity to define and shape their legacy in diverse and meaningful ways. This can encompass a range of contributions, from charitable giving and philanthropy to passing down knowledge and values to future generations. Creating a legacy is about ensuring that the values, causes, and passions that define one's life continue to have a positive influence long after one's passing. For single women, this endeavor can be particularly empowering, offering a sense of purpose and connection that transcends the individual and resonates with the broader community.

In considering how to leave a legacy, it is important to reflect on personal passions, values, and the areas where one's efforts can make the most significant difference. Whether through financial contributions, volunteer work, or mentoring, single women can create a legacy that reflects their deepest commitments and beliefs. By strategically planning how to allocate time, resources, and knowledge, it is possible to build a legacy that not only honors one's life but also supports and uplifts others. This process involves thoughtful consideration of the various avenues available for legacy building and an understanding of how to maximize the impact of one's contributions. Through careful planning and intentional action, single women can leave a legacy that brings lasting change and inspires future generations.

Charitable Giving and Philanthropy: How to Get Involved

Charitable giving and philanthropy provide powerful avenues for single women to leave a meaningful legacy. By supporting causes that align with personal values, women can make a substantial difference in their communities and the world at large. Getting involved in philanthropy can take many forms, from direct financial contributions to active participation in nonprofit organizations. The first step in this journey is to identify the causes that resonate most deeply. This might include areas such as education, healthcare, environmental conservation, social justice, or the arts. Reflecting on personal experiences and passions can help pinpoint where one's contributions can have the most profound impact.

Once a cause is chosen, researching reputable organizations that align with these values is crucial. Look for nonprofits with a clear mission, transparent financial practices, and a track record of making a tangible difference. Donating to such organizations ensures that contributions are used effectively and responsibly. In addition to monetary donations, many nonprofits welcome volunteers and board members. By offering time and expertise, single women can further enhance their impact. Serving on the board of a nonprofit organization or participating in fundraising events are excellent ways to deepen involvement and influence the direction of charitable efforts.

Creating a philanthropic plan can help structure charitable giving and ensure that contributions are consistent and impactful. This plan might include setting up a donor-advised fund, which allows for charitable donations to be made and managed in a tax-advantaged way. Another option is establishing a charitable trust or foundation, providing a more structured and enduring method of giving. These vehicles not only facilitate ongoing support for chosen causes but also offer opportunities for more strategic and large-scale philanthropy. For those interested in leaving a legacy through philanthropy, working with financial advisors and estate planners can help design a giving strategy that aligns with long-term financial goals and legacy aspirations.

Additionally, fostering a culture of giving within one's community can amplify the impact of charitable efforts. Encouraging friends, colleagues, and community members to support the same causes creates a network of like-minded individuals who collectively make a greater difference. Hosting fundraising events, starting charitable initiatives, or simply sharing information about worthy causes can inspire others to join in the effort. Through these actions, single women can create a ripple effect, extending their legacy of generosity and compassion far beyond their individual contributions.

Making a Lasting Impact Through Your Investments and Assets

Investments and assets provide another powerful means for single women to leave a lasting legacy. By strategically directing financial resources, it is possible to support causes and initiatives that align with personal values and have a meaningful impact. Socially responsible investing (SRI) is one approach that allows investors to generate financial returns while also fostering positive social or environmental outcomes. This type of investing involves selecting companies and funds that prioritize ethical practices, sustainability, and social responsibility. By choosing to invest in businesses that align with their values, single women can support corporate practices that contribute to a better world.

Impact investing takes this concept a step further, targeting investments in companies, organizations, and funds with the explicit intention of generating measurable social and environmental benefits alongside financial returns. This approach allows investors to support innovations and projects that directly address pressing global challenges, such as renewable energy, affordable housing, healthcare access, and education. Through impact investing, single women can channel their financial resources into ventures that not only provide potential economic gains but also drive significant positive change.

Real estate investments can also be utilized to leave a legacy. Purchasing property to support affordable housing initiatives or community development projects can make a substantial difference in the lives of many. For example, investing in properties that provide safe and affordable housing for low-income families or senior citizens helps address critical housing shortages and contributes to community stability. Alternatively, donating real estate to charitable organizations can offer them valuable assets to support their missions, whether by using the property directly or selling it to fund their programs.

Estate planning is another key component of using assets to leave a legacy. Creating a comprehensive estate plan ensures that assets are distributed according to one's wishes, supporting chosen causes and providing for loved ones. This might include setting up charitable bequests in a will, designating beneficiaries for retirement accounts and life insurance policies, or establishing trusts to manage and disburse funds over time. By thoughtfully planning the allocation of assets, single women can ensure that their legacy reflects their values and continues to support meaningful endeavors long after they are gone.

Moreover, mentoring the next generation of investors can amplify the impact of legacy building through investments. Sharing knowledge about socially responsible investing, financial planning, and philanthropy with younger individuals helps instill these values and practices early on. By educating and inspiring others to consider the social and environmental implications of their investments, single women can create a legacy of responsible and impactful financial stewardship that extends well into the future.

Passing Down Knowledge and Values to the Next Generation

Leaving a legacy is not solely about financial contributions and investments; it also involves passing down knowledge and values to future generations. This transfer of wisdom and ethical principles can have a profound and enduring impact, shaping the perspectives and actions of those who follow. Single women have the opportunity to influence younger individuals by sharing their experiences, lessons learned, and values cultivated over a lifetime. Whether through formal mentoring, writing, or simply engaging in meaningful conversations, this act of sharing can create a ripple effect, inspiring others to carry forward the principles and causes that mattered most to them.

Mentoring is a powerful way to pass down knowledge and values. By guiding and supporting younger individuals in their personal and professional development, single women can impart valuable skills, insights, and ethical frameworks. This mentorship can take many forms, from career guidance and academic support to life coaching and moral leadership. Effective mentors listen, encourage, and challenge their mentees, fostering growth and resilience. By building strong, trusting relationships, mentors create a lasting influence that extends beyond their immediate interactions, shaping the mentees' decisions and actions for years to come.

Writing is another impactful medium for leaving a legacy of knowledge and values. Authoring books, articles, or personal memoirs allows for the documentation and dissemination of life lessons, wisdom, and values. These written works can serve as enduring resources for family, friends, and even broader audiences. Through storytelling, single women can illustrate how their values guided their actions and decisions, offering readers both inspiration and practical guidance. Writing also allows for the preservation of cultural, familial, or community histories, ensuring that important stories and traditions are remembered and honored.

Engaging in meaningful conversations with family, friends, and community members can also be a powerful way to share knowledge and values. These conversations provide opportunities to discuss important topics, share experiences, and explore ethical dilemmas together. By fostering open, honest dialogue, single women can influence the perspectives and values of those around them. These discussions can help younger individuals navigate their own lives with greater awareness and intentionality, informed by the wisdom of those who came before them.

In addition to these direct methods, creating educational programs or scholarships can also be an effective way to pass down knowledge and values. Establishing scholarships for students pursuing fields related to personal passions or values ensures that future generations have the support they need to make a difference. Educational programs, whether through formal institutions or community-based initiatives, can provide valuable learning opportunities that reflect the legacy builder's commitments and beliefs. By investing in education, single women can help cultivate a generation of informed, ethical, and motivated individuals ready to contribute positively to society.

Ultimately, leaving a legacy as a single woman involves a multifaceted approach that combines financial contributions, investments, and the sharing of knowledge and values. By thoughtfully considering how to engage in philanthropy, direct investments, and personal mentorship, it is possible to create a lasting impact that honors one's life and passions. Through these efforts, single women can ensure that their influence endures, inspiring and supporting future generations to continue the work of creating a better, more just, and compassionate world.

Volunteerism and Giving Back in Retirement

Volunteerism can be one of the most rewarding paths to fulfillment and meaning in retirement, especially for single women seeking purpose and connection. During this stage of life, the desire to make a positive impact in the world often grows stronger, as individuals may find themselves with more time and freedom to explore new interests and invest in the well-being of their communities. Giving back through volunteer work allows retirees to engage in causes they are passionate about, contribute their skills, and make a difference in ways that transcend financial or material considerations. For single women, who may be especially eager to build connections and contribute meaningfully, volunteerism serves as a conduit to forge lasting relationships, support others, and experience personal growth.

Volunteering also provides an opportunity to foster self-discovery and redefine one's identity beyond past roles in careers or family. By dedicating time to causes that resonate with personal values, single retirees can find renewed purpose and a sense of belonging within a community of like-minded individuals. Volunteer work not only benefits those served but also brings immense satisfaction to the giver, who can witness firsthand the impact of their contributions. This reciprocal relationship between volunteer and community creates an enriching experience for all involved, allowing single retirees to leave a positive mark on the world while simultaneously growing in empathy, understanding, and inner strength.

Finding Purpose Through Service

Many single women entering retirement search for a sense of purpose that aligns with their values and passions, and volunteerism often provides a powerful avenue for achieving this. Service connects people to something larger than themselves, offering a sense of significance that enhances emotional well-being and fosters inner peace. Whether by volunteering at a local shelter, participating in environmental conservation efforts, or assisting organizations that support vulnerable populations, service helps retirees channel their experiences, skills, and time into meaningful work that benefits society.

The pursuit of purpose through volunteer work is often linked to greater mental and emotional health in retirement, as studies have shown that individuals who engage in altruistic activities experience lower levels of depression and anxiety. Volunteering builds a sense of accomplishment, a crucial factor for retirees navigating life transitions. This pursuit encourages retirees to use their accumulated skills in a new capacity, revitalizing their sense of identity and personal value. Retirement can be an ideal time to explore new forms of service that may have been impractical or impossible to pursue in earlier years, due to time or family constraints.

Additionally, service brings structure and a rewarding rhythm to life in retirement. Rather than viewing retirement as an indefinite period of relaxation, retirees who engage in volunteer work often report that they enjoy having a routine and a reason to get involved regularly. The activities they choose can vary widely, accommodating each retiree's physical abilities, interests, and energy levels. Volunteering might range from helping organize events to supporting administrative tasks in a nonprofit, participating in outdoor conservation, or even online mentoring programs. No matter the level of commitment, each role offers the chance to establish meaningful goals and attain a sense of accomplishment in a new and rewarding environment.

Becoming a Mentor: Sharing Your Knowledge and Skills

Becoming a mentor in retirement is another powerful way to give back while creating strong, lasting connections with others. As a mentor, a retiree has the chance to share their unique expertise, life lessons, and personal insights, offering valuable guidance to individuals at different stages of life. For single women in particular, mentorship offers a pathway to leave a legacy by empowering the next generation to pursue their goals with clarity and confidence. Mentoring helps bridge generational divides, builds understanding, and brings invaluable wisdom to those who seek guidance on their own life paths.

Mentorship relationships can take various forms, from career-related guidance to personal development coaching. Many professional organizations and nonprofit groups offer mentorship programs that match experienced individuals with those eager to learn, such as young adults entering the workforce, aspiring entrepreneurs, or students pursuing specific career goals. In these settings, mentors can provide practical advice on navigating industries, managing work-life balance, and overcoming challenges. Mentoring also provides a platform for transferring knowledge that might otherwise be lost, preserving the insights and hard-won lessons of one's professional and personal journey.

In addition to formal mentorship opportunities, retirees can offer guidance informally through community programs or individual connections. Volunteering in schools, after-school programs, and youth centers provides countless chances to support younger individuals. Mentoring doesn't always require extensive time commitments; it can be as simple as attending a few sessions per month, sharing encouragement, and providing perspective on challenges that younger generations may face. Through mentoring, retirees not only help others avoid potential pitfalls but also celebrate their own accomplishments by passing on what they have learned. This process creates a fulfilling cycle, where the mentor's journey continues to impact others in positive ways, long after their own goals have been achieved.

Mentorship in retirement offers reciprocal rewards, as the mentor gains a sense of purpose and joy from witnessing the growth of their mentees. This emotional enrichment bolsters the mentor's sense of identity and relevance, providing comfort and pride in seeing how their guidance helps others flourish. Mentees often express deep gratitude, viewing their mentors as role models who inspire them to reach new heights. Thus, through mentorship, single retirees can contribute to a legacy of resilience, perseverance, and kindness, cultivating a profound influence that can last for years to come.

Volunteering Opportunities at Home and Abroad

Retirees today have access to an unprecedented range of volunteer opportunities, both locally and globally, allowing them to engage in meaningful work regardless of location or skill set. Local volunteer options often include involvement in community programs, such as assisting at food banks, animal shelters, libraries, and senior centers. Retirees might also volunteer with local environmental groups, helping with beach clean-ups, tree planting, or nature preservation projects. Community-focused volunteer work allows individuals to make a tangible difference in their immediate surroundings, fostering a sense of connection to their neighborhoods and cities.

In addition to local service, many retirees are exploring volunteer opportunities abroad, which offer unique ways to immerse themselves in different cultures while contributing to meaningful causes. International volunteer programs often focus on areas such as healthcare, education, and community development, providing opportunities for retirees to use their skills to make a significant difference in communities in need. For example, retired teachers might volunteer to teach English in developing countries, while those with medical expertise could assist in clinics or health education initiatives. Some retirees choose to participate in conservation projects in diverse ecosystems, working to preserve wildlife habitats or support sustainable agricultural practices.

Several organizations specialize in coordinating volunteer opportunities for retirees, making it easier to find programs that align with specific interests and abilities. Programs like the Peace Corps and Habitat for Humanity offer structured international experiences, allowing retirees to work within established frameworks and communities. These programs often provide training, accommodations, and support, making it simpler for retirees to focus on their contributions without worrying about logistical concerns. Many of these organizations welcome retirees, as they bring a wealth of experience, stability, and dedication that enrich the volunteer teams.

When exploring international volunteer options, it is essential to consider one's health, comfort with travel, and the specific requirements of each program. Some assignments may be physically demanding or require adjustments to different climates, diets, and cultural norms. However, for those who embrace these challenges, volunteering abroad provides a unique chance to broaden perspectives, engage in meaningful cultural exchange, and form bonds with people from diverse backgrounds. By stepping out of their comfort zones, retirees can experience personal growth while making a real difference in the lives of others.

Volunteering, both at home and abroad, serves as a pathway to adventure, fulfillment, and purpose in retirement. For single women, this endeavor fosters resilience and adaptability, as well as a sense of belonging within various communities. Through these contributions, retirees often find that they gain as much as they give, discovering renewed vitality and satisfaction in their service. Whether through local initiatives or international programs, volunteerism offers a rewarding way to enrich life, strengthen connections, and create a legacy that extends far beyond retirement.

Conclusion

As retirement approaches, single women have a unique opportunity to design a life that truly reflects their values, aspirations, and goals. Embracing this next chapter with confidence and independence can be a deeply empowering experience, especially when equipped with the knowledge and strategies to navigate the challenges of retirement planning. With careful preparation, single women can ensure that their retirement years are filled with security, joy, and a sense of purpose, creating a legacy that will extend far beyond financial security.

This journey begins with a strong foundation of understanding one's personal financial situation and establishing clear, achievable retirement goals. Once these are defined, strategic planning becomes the key to turning them into reality. Whether it's budgeting effectively, reducing debt, or building wealth through smart investments, the right approach can ensure that retirement is not only financially stable but also emotionally fulfilling. A detailed understanding of retirement accounts, social security, and other benefits plays a pivotal role in securing financial well-being, while additional tools like health insurance, life insurance, and long-term care coverage help to protect against unforeseen circumstances.

Equally important is the emphasis on health and wellness. A holistic approach to physical, mental, and emotional well-being ensures that retirement is a time for vitality, exploration, and personal growth. Maintaining an active lifestyle, nurturing social connections, and seeking out new experiences allow retirees to live fulfilling lives, with greater resilience and flexibility to adapt to the inevitable changes that arise. In addition, creating a strong support system of trusted advisors and a network of friends, mentors, and community groups can be invaluable for maintaining the balance and emotional strength necessary for a satisfying retirement. The chance to volunteer, give back, and leave a legacy provides additional layers of meaning, purpose, and contribution to the world.

Retirement is often viewed as the culmination of a long career and years of hard work, but it can also be the beginning of a new and exciting phase of life. Single women have the opportunity to redefine their purpose, seek new adventures, and make lasting contributions to the world around them. By planning effectively, staying engaged, and embracing the freedom that retirement offers, single women can enter this phase with confidence, knowing that they are prepared to live the life they've always dreamed of.

Embracing the Next Chapter with Confidence and Independence

The transition into retirement presents single women with a rare chance to step into a new phase of life that is defined by autonomy, independence, and the freedom to live on one's own terms. While many might associate retirement with the end of an era, it can actually represent the beginning of a more vibrant and fulfilling journey. For women who have spent years building careers, raising families, or managing complex lives, retirement offers an opportunity to reimagine what their days can look like. Whether traveling, pursuing hobbies, or giving back through volunteerism, the next chapter can be filled with as much—or more—purpose and adventure than the years prior.

At the heart of this transition is the confidence that comes from knowing that retirement planning has been thoughtfully executed. Single women, often accustomed to being self-reliant, may find that this phase of life provides the space to fully embrace their autonomy. The financial security built through diligent savings, investments, and smart budgeting allows for the freedom to make choices based on what is truly fulfilling, rather than out of necessity. This sense of independence is one of the greatest rewards of retirement planning and sets the stage for a life lived authentically and intentionally.

To embrace retirement with confidence, it's essential to focus not only on the financial aspects but also on the emotional and social dimensions of this next phase. It's a time to acknowledge all the personal growth and resilience accumulated over a lifetime and use that to shape the retirement years in a way that feels meaningful. Single women can enjoy the independence that retirement affords, while also creating opportunities for connection, personal growth, and service to others. Taking care of one's health, cultivating new relationships, and finding meaningful ways to engage with the world provide a well-rounded and satisfying retirement experience.

Key Takeaways for a Secure and Satisfying Solo Retirement

A secure and satisfying solo retirement is achievable for single women who are proactive in their approach to planning. One of the most important takeaways is the need to develop a clear and comprehensive financial plan. This includes understanding your income needs, creating a sustainable budget, and saving aggressively to ensure a comfortable lifestyle throughout retirement. Reducing debt and focusing on wealth-building through investments and other assets can contribute to long-term financial security. Whether through a 401(k), IRAs, or other retirement accounts, understanding the available options and how they align with one's financial goals is crucial for building a stable foundation.

Equally important is the emotional and social aspect of retirement planning. Single women must recognize that retirement is not just about finances but about maintaining mental, physical, and emotional well-being. Staying active, eating well, and nurturing social relationships are essential components of a fulfilling retirement. A support network of family, friends, and advisors can help provide guidance and encouragement, while engagement in meaningful activities and volunteerism can create a lasting sense of purpose. Additionally, for women who are passionate about leaving a legacy, volunteering, philanthropy, and passing on knowledge and wisdom can offer powerful ways to create an impact in the world.

Another key takeaway is the importance of living a balanced life. It is easy to focus solely on finances and overlook the equally critical aspects of social connection, wellness, and personal fulfillment. By considering the whole picture of retirement, single women can create a retirement lifestyle that is rich in experiences, relationships, and opportunities for growth. This balanced approach ensures that retirement is not just about financial security but about living a life of meaning and joy.

Final Words of Encouragement for Single Women Planning Retirement

Retirement may seem like a distant milestone, but for single women who take the time to plan thoughtfully, it can be a time of great freedom, independence, and joy. The path to a secure retirement is not without its challenges, but with careful attention to financial planning, health, and social well-being, single women can navigate this transition with confidence. The key is to begin early, set clear goals, and remain committed to achieving those goals. Each woman's retirement journey will look different, but the principles of smart financial planning, health maintenance, and meaningful engagement apply universally.

For those who feel overwhelmed by the process, it is important to remember that it's never too late to start planning. Seeking professional advice from financial planners, legal advisors, and healthcare professionals can provide invaluable guidance and ensure that all aspects of retirement are considered. Embracing this phase of life means embracing all the possibilities it holds. Whether through discovering new hobbies, exploring new places, or building a legacy through service, retirement is an opportunity to live with greater intention and purpose. For single women, this is a time to take ownership of the next chapter, live fully, and create a retirement that is not just financially secure but rich in experiences, relationships, and personal fulfillment.

Retirement is a journey, not a destination. Embrace it with an open heart and a clear plan, and the rewards will be both profound and long-lasting. The future is bright for single women who take control of their retirement planning, and the possibilities are endless for those who are ready to embrace the adventure that awaits.

www.ingramcontent.com/pod-product-compliance
Lightning Source LLC
Chambersburg PA
CBHW071057240526
45471CB00016B/1985